Philip,

Thank you for your trust in HFF — we appreciate the relationship very much.
    Best regards,

        Paul

PS — I would go straight to the "Big & Boogey" section!

TIPSY TEXAN

THIS BOOK IS DEDICATED TO JOE EIFLER

Andrews McMeel Publishing, LLC an Andrews McMeel Universal company 1130 Walnut Street, Kansas City, Missouri 64106.

www.andrewsmcmeel.com

14 15 16 17 SDB 10 9 8 7 6 5 4 3 2

ISBN: 978-1-4494-2420-6

Library of Congress Control Number: 2013930081

Cover and interior design by Randall Lockridge/Terrace Partners

Photography by Michael Thad Carter: pages 42, 94, 102, 122, 150, and 174
Photography by AMAC Solutions: page 195
Photography by Bob Stickney: page 15
Photography courtesy of iStockphoto.com: pages 41, 56, 68, and the flag on the cover.
Cover and all other photography by Aimee Wenske
Food styling by Kate LeSueur
Drink illustrations by Lee Newton

www.tipsytexan.com

ATTENTION: SCHOOLS AND BUSINESSES
Andrews McMeel books are available at quantity discounts with bulk purchase for educational, business, or sales promotional use. For information, please e-mail the Andrews McMeel Special Sales Department: specialsales@amuniversal.com

TIPSY TEXAN

SPIRITS AND COCKTAILS FROM THE LONE STAR STATE

DAVID ALAN

PHOTOGRAPHY BY
AIMEE WENSKE AND MICHAEL THAD CARTER

Andrews McMeel
Publishing, LLC
Kansas City • Sydney • London

CONTENTS

INTRODUCTION

When I set out to write a book on Texas cocktails and spirits, it was not immediately apparent where I should begin. Unlike Kentucky, we don't have an indigenous spirit that defines us. Unlike New York, we don't have any ancient taverns where the Founding Fathers might have watered their troops. We don't have an uninterrupted tie to the cocktail's past, like New Orleans, and our modern cocktail bars are still too new to have established a regional style of their own. Tragically, our "national beer"—Lone Star—is owned by a Russian company, and our favorite cocktail, the Margarita, most likely wasn't invented here.

So, where do we start?

Regionally speaking, Texas is a melting-pot state. We are Southern, but not deeply so. It is a southwestern state, but not all chile-peppers-and-Navajo-rugs like New Mexico. All of those Louisiana expats slipping across the Sabine River have left their mark on our cuisine and our drinking habits, especially around Houston and parts east. Most important, we're hugely influenced by our neighbors to the south. Texas cuisine is inextricably linked to the traditions of the millions of Mexicans, Mexican Americans, and Tejanos who populate the state, who have always populated the state. (Recall that the border used to be located several hundred miles to the north, and that one of the proverbial "six flags" that flew over Texas is that of Mexico.) We have a very visible and revered rural heritage, and yet our modern cities (including six of the largest twenty in the United States) attract people from across the country, and from around the world.

I have tried to honor all of those influences here.

I'm a big believer in the local food community. Although we have the luxury as modern humans to force our agenda on the food supply and obtain anything we want at any time of year, I don't recommend it. A local watermelon at the peak of season is a thing of incomparable beauty—in the heat of an August sun, nothing is more refreshing, especially in a Watermelon Mojito (page 90). Texas grapefruits, erupting with juicy sweetness, will put to shame any out-of-state grapefruit. We should rejoice in that, and when they're gone, they're gone until next season, giving us something to look forward to.

Texas is fortunate to have virtually year-round growing seasons, and with a few exceptions we can grow just about anything here. Throughout the book I have highlighted agricultural products that thrive in Texas, especially those that are native or adaptive. Nature tells us what she wants us to eat (or drink!) and when, if we only listen.

Thanks to the trailblazing efforts of Tito Beveridge and those who have followed in his footsteps, we have a local spirits industry to rally around. In this book you will meet Tito; go on a picnic with the first lady distiller in Texas, Paula Angerstein; and behold the majestic beard of Waco whiskey distiller Chip Tate.

The recipes in this book are meant to be simple enough that most people can make them with a relatively basic home bar and a few tools. There are recipes from a number of prominent Texas bartenders, such as Austin's Bill Norris, and Houston's Bobby Heugel. Some of these are simple, and some are more mixological, but they all represent what Texas bartenders are making at this juncture in time. I have also included a number of my favorite classic cocktails; for many of these I offer simple variations that include local produce or flavors, such as the Fig Daiquiri (page 52).

In many families, culinary indoctrination of the next generation starts at a young age. I recall making fried pies and stamping cookies in my grandmother's kitchen as a child. The ever-present Fry Daddy on her counter no doubt contributed to my present-day obsession with chicken wings. Unfortunately she did not teach me how to make a Martini. Like most young people, I learned how to imbibe

On the Organization of the Recipes

Some cocktail books are organized alphabetically, and some are organized by the base spirit of the cocktail. It was my goal to organize the recipes by the way people actually drink—thinking that most people don't get a craving just for a specific spirit, but for a cocktail that is cool and refreshing, or potent and bold, be it made from gin, whiskey, or tequila. The recipes in this book are organized by the style and personality of the drink. The Light, Bright, and Refreshing drinks are the thirst-quenchers for our hot summer season. Big & Boozy recipes are for spirit-driven, higher-octane cocktails to be enjoyed when the heat recedes and the sun goes down.

Sweet, Creamy & Desserty drinks will satisfy your sweet tooth. As with all recipes, these are meant to be guidelines and not etched-in-stone rules. Every palate is different, and every ingredient is different—especially when you're dealing with fresh seasonal produce. I recommend that you follow the recipe first, taste the cocktail, and adjust to your liking. Each recipe makes one cocktail unless otherwise noted.

Where the origin of a drink is known, or if there is a particular inspiration or influence for a drink, I have attempted to state it. The history of cocktails and spirits is by its nature a fuzzy one, and any omission or misinterpretation is unintentional.

from people who didn't know what they were doing. I remember the first drink I learned how to order in a bar—it was a Cape Cod. Before that, the first "cocktail" I ever learned to make included the F-word in its name and a can of frozen grape juice in its recipe. (For all of our sake, neither of these treasures is included in this book.)

The process of learning how to drink like an adult is so often a self-guided one. This book is by no means a complete education. But I hope you will approach it with the same curiosity and sense of humor with which we approach mixing and drinking drinks at Tipsy Manor.

A BRIEF HISTORY
OF THE AMERICAN COCKTAIL

The mixing of drinks dates back to time immemorial, with recipes in all manner of ancient texts for drinks to cure what ails you. The history of the cocktail, by contrast, is comparatively modern. Our colonial forebears came to these shores with plenty of intoxicating cargo, but only rudimentary ideas for mixed drinks—lightly alcoholic drinks such as syllabubs, caudles, and flips that were rich in calories from eggs and milk. Punch was a noteworthy exception and reigned supreme over the pre-cocktails. Within one hundred years of the nation's founding, however, a wildly innovative, distinctly American cocktail cuisine would emerge and begin to be exported to points far and wide—an alcoholic ambassador from the fledgling United States.

We are once again in a golden age of the cocktail, with Texas cities finally catching up with our coastal counterparts in the mixological arts—even the punch bowl has been dislodged from the top shelf, dusted off, and returned to its rightful place on the bar. As we pay homage to the contemporary renaissance of artisanal beverages, let us first take a survey of the cocktail's modern history.

In colonial America, the idea of the individual drink had not yet taken hold. Communal drinking was the norm, punch was often drunk straight from the bowl, and toasting to health was widespread. Those were bibulous times, with per capita consumption many times higher than it is today. Not only was it uncommon (even unhealthy) to drink straight water, it was considered pitiable by some commentators. Much community activity centered around the tavern, and the tavern centered around the punch bowl. To the modern eye, one of the first things we notice when looking at engravings of these old "bars" is that there is no bar—customers sat around tables, facing one another. They did not sit at a long counter facing the bartender, because that person had not yet emerged as a professional distinct from the multifaceted tavern keeper of yore.

As the young nation began to industrialize and urbanize in the nineteenth century, drinking habits likewise evolved. It was not unusual for apprentices and masters working in small shops to go through much of their day under some kind of mild inebriation. Alcohol was a good source of calories—fermentation and distillation are above all else a means of preserving grain and fruit. Likewise, before the advent of modern purification techniques, alcohol was added to water for its antibacterial qualities. This all changed as the factory system developed. Whereas a few men can safely sit in a workshop making saddles under the influence, the game changes when hundreds or thousands of people have to work in close proximity, around expensive (and dangerous) manufacturing equipment. It is no coincidence that it was not just religionists who were the most vocal proponents of Prohibition, but also industrialists such as John D. Rockefeller.

The evolution of the commercial ice trade was also a major contributor to the emergence of cocktails and professional bartenders. Whereas ice had previously been available as a luxury for the wealthy, the development of sophisticated harvesting, storage, and transportation techniques by Frederick "the Ice King" Tudor enabled the democratization and spread of ice. Cut in winter from northern ponds, lakes, and rivers, huge blocks of ice were shipped in insulated cargo vessels to ports as far away as New Orleans, Havana, and Calcutta. New tools and techniques were developed to incorporate ice into drinks, and with them countless recipes, many of which were collected in the first known drinks book to be published in the United States, *The Bar-Tender's Guide* (1862), by Jerry Thomas. The age of the cocktail bartender was born, and many of the modern tools and major recipes that are in use today were developed by the closing decades of the nineteenth century.

However, the cocktail party didn't last long as the Women's Christian Temperance Union (WCTU), the largest and most powerful women's organization of its time, advocated for temperance, not complete abstinence—moderation, not abolition. But temperance evolved into a full-on prohibition movement with the emergence of such single-issue parties as the Anti-Saloon League. The ASL was so effective at making it untenable for a politician to be publicly wet that both major political parties added Prohibition to their respective platforms by 1918. The Eighteenth Amendment was ratified by the states on January 16, 1919, and went into effect the following year, thus beginning the thirteen-year drought known euphemistically as the Noble Experiment.

Prohibition largely failed at its main objective of drying out the nation. It gave a mammoth boost to organized crime and made criminals out of ordinary citizens. Whereas Prohibition was a monolithic, complete effort that was national in scope, repeal was the opposite: piecemeal, fractional, and hyperlocalized in scope. The Twenty-first Amendment threw the decision to the states, many of which in turn passed the responsibility on to counties, cities, and even justice-of-the-peace precincts—hence the incredible patchwork quilt of liquor regulations that result in different degrees of "wet" virtually every place you go. The entire state of Mississippi was bone dry until 1966. Many readers will remember when you couldn't buy liquor by the drink in Texas, and as of this printing the denizens of Tyler still have to leave the city limits to buy a bottle—one of the many lingering effects of Prohibition.

The middle decades of the twentieth century were for the most part an unfortunate time for American cocktail mixology, the profession emerging from Prohibition in a state one might predict it would be in, having been forced underground, unable to evolve for over a decade. We went from exporting our ideas and traditions about cocktails to exporting the very talent, as professional barmen sought wetter pastures abroad. Others left the business entirely, or continued to practice the craft in illegal speakeasies, working with whatever ingredients they could get hold of.

One exception to the general malaise of mid-century mixology was the tiki movement. Tiki was a glorious pastiche of tropical and Asian design aesthetics conjured by Hollywood, pioneered by such colorful characters as Don the Beachcomber and "Trader Vic" Bergeron. The tiki bars offered a cuisine of cocktails based on tropical flavors, but built in a classical fashion with balance and complexity in mind, and practitioners of the art were massively successful. In the 1930s, the early tiki bars and restaurants offered a Technicolor culinary fantasia against the black-and-white backdrop of the recent Depression; a decade later, they offered solace to the souls of weary soldiers and provided an escape to citizens. With countless soldiers returning from the Pacific theater, and with the popularization of Hawaiian tourism (and eventual statehood), an increased interest in the South Pacific manifested itself across the middlebrow culture of the day. Americans had now been exposed to the allure of the Orient, and "Polynesian Pop" took the country by storm. What started in the backyard of Hollywood in the 1930s had spread

by the 1950s such that one could escape to the tropics in just about any city in America—everything from shopping malls to home decor soon benefited from a touch of the islands.

Whereas tiki palaces provided the most flamboyant means of escape, the most common sanctuary was the home itself. As Elaine Tyler May writes in *Homeward Bound*, "The home seemed to offer a secure private nest removed from the dangers of the outside world." Seeking respite from the din of war, the deprivation of the Depression, and the chaos of crowded cities, Americans flocked to the countryside to populate it with suburbs. America flexed its industrial might in a mind-boggling collusion of developers and homebuilders, automobile manufacturers, tire makers, and road-building contractors, all supported by government will and the GI Bill. In a short time, suburbanization forever changed the American landscape, and it also changed the way we drink.

As Americans strived to escape the chaos of the city for the calm of the suburbs, our drinking habits changed. Without the convenience of the corner tavern or neighborhood pub, we saw the rise of the home bartender and an explosion of gear catering toward that emerging market. Whereas cocktail manuals from before Prohibition were sparse guidebooks for working professionals, those that emerged afterward were lush with detailed descriptions and images. Ted Saucier's *Bottoms Up* (1951) featured pinup gals from the brushes of America's top commercial illustrators; *Esquire* magazine's *Handbook for Hosts* (1949) offered not just an elaborate selection of cocktail recipes but also meat-carving tips, jokes, toasts, and rules for canasta and bridge.

At the same time as these new backyard bons vivants emerge, so, too, did the perfect spirit for those with rudimentary drink-making skills. In the early history of American drink, vodka was either a nonentity or what might be considered an ethnic specialty, an oddity such as slivovitz or rompope consumed not by the masses but only by isolated demographic groups. So unknown was vodka, in the early years Smirnoff marketed it as "white whiskey," as a way of speaking to the brown spirit that was the dominant hooch in mid-century America. Smirnoff's use of popular culture was masterful—the biggest stars of the day appeared in their ads, and James Bond's method of ordering the vodka martini is no doubt the most famous cocktail order of all time.

Vodka flourished by the 1960s and outpaced gin as the most-consumed clear spirit in the United States; ten years later it would eclipse bourbon as best-selling spirit, a position that it still holds today. In just a few short decades, vodka forever changed the trajectory of American cocktail mixology. Since vodka's neutral profile takes on the flavor of whatever it is mixed with, the cold war–era cocktails were simple to make and easy to drink—the perfect beverage component to a nation whose food system had become largely industrialized and palate bland.

The landscape for beverages remained bleak throughout the 1970s and '80s, but during this time, the foundation was being laid for what ultimately would result in the cocktail and spirit renaissance whose throes we currently occupy. What is good for the kitchen is good for the bar, and so the work of natural foods pioneers such as Alice Waters helped create the space in which artisanal beverage producers would later flourish. In the late 1980s and 1990s, a few American bartenders, notably New York's Dale DeGroff, started to excavate traditional recipes and techniques that had largely disappeared from the mainstream culture.

The cocktail has once again regained a distinguished place in the American culinary conversation. The esteemed James Beard Foundation now confers its honors upon top talents not just in the kitchen but also behind the bar. And it is now difficult to find a new chef-driven restaurant of any worth that has not given serious consideration to its cocktail menu.

If the narrative of American cocktails and spirits has mostly been told from a coastal perspective, Texas is finally getting its due. Cocktails and cocktail culture have traveled inward from such markets as San Francisco, Portland, and New York to such cities as Austin and San Antonio; in the next wave we will see these people and concepts expand outward from urban cores to the suburbs. Two of my favorite cocktail dens that have opened in recent years are Whiskey Cake (Plano) and 400 Rabbits (Circle C, Austin); both operate not in hip, restored warehouse districts but in suburban strip malls.

Inasmuch as consumer enthusiasm for cocktails has skyrocketed in recent years, there has also been increased sophistication on the production side. More artisanal distillates are now on the shelf than at any point in modern memory. Craft distilling is in full bloom, with small-scale distilleries making an

impact for the first time since before Prohibition (there are over 50 licensed distilleries in Texas, up from zero in the mid-1990s, when Tito Beveridge started distilling his local vodka). Craft brewing, which had experienced a boom in Texas in the 1990s, is going through another growth spurt in Austin, with nearly a dozen new breweries coming online in as many months. Almost eighty years after its repeal, Prohibition continues to unravel, with "local option" elections making more and more communities safe for alcohol. The ranks of cocktail aficionados, both amateur and professional, continue to swell— Texas, once a cocktail underdog, now represents one of the largest single-state delegations to Tales of the Cocktail, the international cocktail festival held in New Orleans each summer. Never one to be a shrinking violet, Texas is finally on the mixology map. ❧

TOOLS AND TECHNIQUES

GLASSWARE GUIDE

Although glassware is often an afterthought to many people's cocktail preparation, it's important not to fall into this trap. The glass is the costume in which your cocktail performs—you must make sure that your drinks are properly wardrobed.

 Cocktail glass—This V-shaped glass is commonly referred to as a "Martini" glass, and has been an iconic symbol of liquid merriment since at least the middle of the twentieth century. Unfortunately, the glass has lost its way over the last several decades, as it has ballooned in size to accommodate all manner of fruity 'tini drinks that bear no resemblance to the classic Martini. A properly sized cocktail glass should be made of thin glass—crystal is nice—without the "rolled" edge around the rim, and it should hold not more than 6 ounces of liquid. Make sure the glass is clear, so as to show off the beautiful cocktail you've crafted.

 Highball—A highball glass—straight sided and containing 10 to 12 ounces—is great for giving an upscale feel to simple "one-plus-one" drinks such as Bourbon & Ginger.

 Collins glass—Like a stretched-out highball glass, a Collins glass is perfect for its eponymous cocktail as well as for Mojitos, swizzles, and all manner of tall, elegant drinks. Holds 12 to 14 ounces.

 Coupe—This round-bottomed, stemmed glass is great for classically proportioned cocktails, especially big and boozy numbers. Coupes are also perfectly suited for egg and egg white drinks. They should accommodate about 4 ounces of liquid.

 Rocks or Old Fashioned glass—An Old Fashioned glass should be short, squatty, and have a fat, heavy base that requires a little bit of muscle to lift. Although it should be sized at 6 to 8 ounces, it will generally be only partially filled, with either a shot of booze on the rocks, or with the glass's namesake cocktail.

 Double Old Fashioned glass—As its name implies, this is a giant rocks glass, though perhaps not quite twice as big at 10 to 12 ounces. It's great for giving a grandiose feel to a pour of neat spirits or spirits on a giant rock. The double Old Fashioned glass is also perfectly sized for full-figured iced drinks such as the Texas Mai Tai (page 184) and El Pepino (page 55).

Julep cup—This small pewter, silver-plated, or sterling silver cup is a staple of the Southern sideboard. The metal acts as a conductor, and the cup frosts up as heat is drawn out of the whiskey and the julep cools. A typical julep cup holds about 10 ounces of liquid. In a pinch, a highball or double Old Fashioned glass is perfectly suitable for making Mint Juleps at home—a julep in the "wrong" glass is better than no julep at all, so don't despair.

 Pint glass—A pint glass, as its name implies, should hold 16 ounces. Generally, pint glasses don't have much use in the actual service of cocktails, but are an essential component of the Boston shaker.

 Punch cup/bowl—Punch bowls are indispensible for entertaining with ease, but they don't have to be complicated. Whether you pick yours up at a thrift store or a modern home decor boutique, don't be shy with it. If you have four people, that is enough to constitute a punch party in my book—you don't have to save it for the holiday party.

 Snail—One of the hallmarks of the tiki era is that in creating their Polynesian fantasia, the tiki pioneers completely upended the glassware protocol of the cocktail bar. No longer would it suffice to have highballs and Old Fashioned and cocktail glasses. The tiki lounge invented a whole new vernacular that included volcano bowls, scorpion bowls, Fog Cutter mugs, and rum "barrels"—all made from ceramic. If you troll secondhand stores and online auctions, you can come up with a treasure trove of tiki gear. I also encourage you to use your imagination here—if it looks like it wants to hold a giant tropical beverage, go all in. Whether it holds half a pint or half a gallon, make it a tiki.

Prepping Glass for Service

Glassware should always be polished clean before service. In most instances it is appropriate to chill the glass, to achieve maximum coldness for the cocktail. The freezer is the ideal placeto chill a glass. If you lack freezer capacity, you can chill a glass by filling it with ice and water for a minute before preparing the cocktail.

MEET YOUR GEAR

Although I have found myself in circumstances that required mixing drinks in the bottom of a vase, using a Tabasco bottle as a muddler, and straining the resulting masterpiece with some kind of undergarment, there is no substitute for having the proper tools. Some tools are essential, some are optional, and some are ridiculous. I have mentioned all here but made an effort to sort them out, at least in my mind, in order of importance. The good news is that you can purchase basic versions of most of the essential tools at a restaurant supply store or kitchen specialty retailer—everything you need to get started will range between thirty and fifty dollars. And you have the rest of your life to collect all the other stuff that you don't need but can't live without.

Essential Bar Kit

- **Shaker**

    o **Boston shaker**—An inexpensive and practical option, the Boston shaker consists of a pint-size mixing glass and shaker tin. Nice because the parts are interchangeable—just about any pint glass or shaker tin will work with another pint glass or mixing tin.

    o **Metal on metal**—A variation on a Boston shaker, but made with two metal tins instead of metal and glass. A standard set generally consists of a pair of shaker tins sized 18 and 28 ounces.

    o **Cobbler**—The three-piece variety consists of a base, a top with a built-in strainer, and a cap. These stylish shakers are very popular in European and Japanese bars, less so in the United States. A "Parisian" shaker looks similar to a cobbler shaker, though it consists of only two pieces and does not have a built-in strainer.

- **Hawthorne strainer**—Used for straining shaken cocktails from a shaker tin. The tighter the spring, the better the straining action.

- **Julep strainer**—Used for straining stirred cocktails from a mixing glass.

- **Bar spoon**—For stirring cocktails and fetching garnishes from the jar.

- **Jiggers**—For ensuring consistent results, accurate pours are essential.

- **Muddler**—Expressing juice from citrus fruits or berries, or bruising herbs.

- **Paring knife**—Essential for cutting fruit and vegetable garnishes.

- **Cutting board**—Plastic boards are nice because they can go through the dishwasher. On the other hand, wooden boards are pretty, especially the very durable ones made from Texas mesquite.

- **Juice squeezer**—The handheld citrus squeezer is adequate for home use; a stand model is necessary for professional applications.

- **Fine-mesh strainer**—Catches bits of fruit or shards of ice that might cloud or clutter your "up" cocktail.

- **Channel knife**—For pulling long twists of citrus fruit rinds. The shallower the V, the less pith you will have in your cocktail.

- **Vegetable peeler**—For removing a wide strip of citrus zest, what is sometimes called a longitudinal or latitudinal zest garnish.

- **Matches or lighter**—For flaming a citrus zest, or lighting a friend's or customer's cigar or cigarette.

- **Wine tool**—For cutting foil and removing corks from wine bottles.

Bar Kit 2.0

All of the components of Essential Bar Kit plus:

- **Nutmeg grater**—For grating nutmeg or cinnamon onto tiki and holiday drinks.

- **Tongs**—For handling garnishes without touching them.

- **Mixing glass with spout**—Although a basic pint glass will get the job done, there is nothing sexier than using an etched mixing glass with a spout, as our colleagues do waaaay across the pond (in Japan).

- **iSi soda siphon**—For carbonating water to spritz into a cocktail, or for even carbonating the cocktail itself.

- **Lewis bag and wooden mallet**—To make crushed ice.

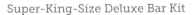

Super-King-Size Deluxe Bar Kit

- **Atomizer**—For dispensing blasts of spirits or bitters to embellish the top of a drink with an aromatic and/or visual finish such as bitters, absinthe, or mezcal. For an extra flourish, you can ignite the spray, though you may have to increase the proof of the liquid in the atomizer with a higher-proof spirit (such as cask-strength whiskey or high-proof rum) to get it to ignite. This technique is especially effective when garnishing an egg white cocktail. Just be sure you don't do this in the direction of any people or furniture that may be injured by flaming liquid; and keep a fire extinguisher handy. The atomizer is also an effective way to "season" a glass, as when you season a Sazerac glass with absinthe (see page 176). Misto is a preferred brand (before they were repurposed by cocktail bartenders, atomizers were more commonly used to spray olive oil).

- **Punch bowl and ladle**

- **Absinthe fountain, glasses, and spoons**

- **iSi whipped cream canister**—For making specialty foams for cocktails.

- **Champagne stoppers**—For preserving leftover bubbly.

- **Microplane**—For grating citrus zest.

- **Blue Blazer mugs**—For making the eponymous flaming drink that must be volleyed back and forth between two silver mugs, while on fire.

- **Silicone ice trays**—For making large or specialized pieces of ice.

- **Cigar cutter**—For the convenience of your cigar-smoking guest or customer.

TECHNIQUES

Garnishes

The function of a garnish is manifold. First and foremost, a garnish should beautify the drink. Like a window without curtains, a garnishless cocktail looks rather naked. Second, the garnish should contribute to the flavor of the drink. It can either draw from or complement flavors already present in a drink, or provide contrast in a pleasing way. Third, a garnish contributes aroma to the cocktail—so that even before you take the first sip, you have an anticipation of what the drink is going to taste like.

- **Herbs**—Always use fresh herbs; it is okay to even keep them attached to the plant if you have the space. Store them in cool water or wrapped in a moist towel in the refrigerator to extend shelf life. The most attractive sprigs and upper leaves should be used for garnishes. The less beauteous ones can still be used to make syrups, or for muddling. To open up herbs' full aroma, give them a quick "spank" by clapping them once between your hands.

- **Citrus Garnishes: Whole Fruit**—It is important to cut garnishes as close to service as possible to prevent their drying out and turning brown.

    o **Wheels**—Citrus wheels are latitudinal slices of citrus fruit, usually lemons and oranges.

    o **Wedges**—Citrus wedges are used both for muddling at the bottom of a drink and for garnishing the top of the drink.

- **Citrus Garnishes: Expressed Citrus Peel**—Citrus-zest garnishes enhance the beauty, aroma, and flavor of a cocktail without changing the balance of the drink, which is a liability with whole-fruit garnishes. When using citrus peels, your goal is to remove the outer zest without capturing the bitter white pith in the process. If you have steady hands, a paring knife will do the trick. Although less graceful, a good sharp veggie peeler provides roughly the same results, more safely. Ideally, position the fruit near the surface of the glass you are garnishing, making sure to aim the spray of oil in the direction of the glass—as the blade cuts through the citrus skin, it sends off a plume of fragrant essential oils.

    o **Lemon "pigtail"**—The classic Martini garnish, made by running a channel knife around the lemon, and wrapping the resulting twist around a bar spoon or other object to tighten its coils.

Lemon "Pigtail"

Citrus Wheel and Wedge

Citrus Strip

Citrus Equator

o **Citrus strip**—Using a paring knife or veggie peeler, take off a strip of peel, going longitudinally from one pole of the fruit to the other. The resulting twist will be approximately the size and shape of an adhesive bandage—about ¾ inch wide by 2½ inches long, depending on the size of the fruit.

o **Lemon or orange coin**—A round disk of citrus peel approximately the size of a quarter.

o **Citrus equator**—As the name implies, a citrus equator is a piece of peel that is taken from the waist of the fruit. These garnishes are great for classic Crustas, tiki-style cocktails, and drinks served over crushed ice, as they can take up the entire rim of a glass.

o **Flamed citrus peel**—Popularized by Dale DeGroff, this technique involves expressing the essential oil of a citrus peel across a flame, thus garnishing the surface of the drink with caramelized essential oil (and providing a bit of a fireworks show, which is always a nice touch).

Shaking, Stirring, Building, and Swizzling

- **Shaking and Stirring**—The two most common methods for chilling a cocktail are stirring and shaking. We generally stir cocktails when they consist only of spirited ingredients—liquors, liqueurs, bitters, fortified wines, and so on. When citrus, muddled fruit, eggs, or cream are involved, we almost always shake the drink. For maximum coldness (and showmanship) it is a good idea to chill your mixing glasses before using them. Whether stirring or shaking, it is important to remember that these techniques serve two functions: First, to chill. A properly chilled cocktail must be very cold. Second, to dilute. Dilution is often viewed as a bad thing, but with a cocktail, proper dilution is critical—in a shaken or stirred cocktail, the resulting beverage will gain an additional 25 to 30 percent of volume from the melted ice. Not enough dilution and your drink is too boozy; too much and it's a watery mess.

o **Stirring**—Stirring should preferably be done in a clear glass mixing container so that the person for whom the drink is being made can behold the full spectacle, which is obscured when you stir a drink in a metal container. When stirring with large, cold ice (such as from a home ice cube tray or KOLD-DRAFT machine), it is best to mix in a few cracked ice cubes. This will increase the surface area of the ice and therefore increase chilling and dilution. All too often, a stirred cocktail is either not cold enough, not dilute enough, or both. Stirring allows you to chill and dilute a cocktail without affecting the drink's clarity. If the technique is executed properly, the drink should pour in silky thick ribbons with no ice chips or bubbles.

○ **Shaking**—Shaking a drink will chill and dilute it with the additional benefit of agitating it into a vigorous emulsion. Properly shaken drinks should be light, lively, and effervescent with an infinite number of tiny bubbles.

- **Building**—If a recipe says to "build" a cocktail, it refers to the practice of crafting the drink directly in the serving glass, as opposed to in a mixing glass or shaking tin. This is done with simple highballs and some drinks that are going to be "swizzled."

- **Swizzling**—The traditional swizzle stick is made of wood and though these are fortunately available now through specialty suppliers, you can accomplish the basic task with a bar spoon. Submerge the swizzle stick partway into your built cocktail and clasp between the palms of your hands. Moving your palms back and forth will agitate the swizzle stick, thus chilling, diluting, and invigorating your cocktail in the process.

- **Rolling**—Sometimes I specify that the drink be "rolled." This involves pouring the contents of the drink, plus ice, back and forth a few times between two mixing containers. This technique is most commonly used with the Bloody Mary because the agitation of shaking such a drink would give it an unpleasantly frothy head.

- **Muddling**—Too often, muddled drinks suffer from being overly muddled. Use the muddler to apply gentle pressure to release aromatics from herbs; use a little more pressure to release juice from citrus wedges or to crush berries. But don't overdo it.

- **Fine straining**—While pouring a cocktail from a Boston shaker into a cocktail glass, hold a fine-mesh strainer between the shaker and the glass. This catches muddled fruit, herbs, and other particles that you don't want clouding up your cocktail.

Ice

Ideally, cocktail ice should be in big, cold, dry chunks, as this allows us to chill a drink as long as possible before it is overly diluted. In reality, we are often dealing with the ice that we were dealt; even with "inferior" small wet ice there are things we can do to maximize its potential. Always strain away any water that the ice might be sitting in. Always use fresh ice for each drink you're stirring or shaking. Lastly, after chilling a drink, always pour the drink over fresh ice in the glass—don't serve the "used" ice from the shaker tin. Imagine ice as having a finite amount of chilling capacity to give you. If you serve used ice, the ice will melt before the drinker is done with the drink, because it has already given up most of its chill.

- **Big ice**—Sometimes size really does matter, and with ice it can definitely be true. If you are a drinker of whiskey on the rocks, for example, you know that one or two large ice cubes is preferable to a bunch of small ones because they keep your whiskey cold without overly diluting it. Certain cocktails, such as the Negroni, look fabulous over one or two giant ice cubes. There is now a variety of inexpensive silicone ice trays for this purpose.

- **Crushed ice**—Crushed ice is essential for such drinks as the Mint Julep. The best way to make it is using a Lewis bag. Fill the canvas bag with whole ice and beat it with an ice mallet, meat tenderizer, heavy muddler, or rolling pin—whatever you have handy. If you need to hold crushed ice for any amount of time, store it in a perforated pan or colander so that melt water can strain off.

- **Punch ice**—The punch bowl is one of those situations where standard ice will just not suffice. Because punch sits out and is drunk over time, small ice will melt too fast—diluting the drink too quickly, and not lasting long enough to keep the punch cold. Only a very large block of ice will both slowly dilute and steadily chill a bowl of punch over time. If you are fortunate enough to have an ice vendor nearby who will supply you with blocks of ice, that is all well and good. For the rest of us, it is necessary to manufacture it ourselves. There are several ways to accomplish this. The easiest is to fill a silicone loaf pan, or a Jell-O mold, with cold water and freeze it overnight. The beauty of this method is that you can freeze sprigs of herbs, edible flowers, or citrus wheels into the ice for beautiful effect. You can also fill a clean paper juice or milk carton or plastic jug and place it in the freezer overnight. For service, cut away the container to reveal a large, solid chunk of ice. A cheater method if you are in need of a large chunk of ice but have forgotten to do it the night before: Fill your mold with standard ice and then fill with water and place in the freezer. This will freeze in a couple of hours as opposed to overnight. Not ideal, but will get the job done!

LIGHT, BRIGHT, AND REFRESHING

ACE OF SPADES

This cocktail combines some of my favorite early summer flavors and is a great reminder that tomatoes are in fact a fruit. Blackberries give the cocktail a stunning color, and the tomato—barely perceptible—lends it a supple mouthfeel.

5 ripe blackberries

1 small tomato wedge, or 1 plump cherry tomato

½ ounce Simple Syrup *(page 83)*

1½ ounces 100% agave silver tequila

½ ounce freshly squeezed lemon juice

Lemon twist, for garnish

In the bottom of a mixing glass, muddle the blackberries, tomato, and simple syrup. Add the tequila and lemon juice and shake vigorously with ice to chill. Strain into a chilled cocktail glass or serve over ice. Garnish with the lemon twist.

DAISY VERDE

This Daisy variation comes from Texas bartender Adam Harris. The pineapple "caramel" came to him by accident. In the process of making pineapple syrup, he walked away from the stove and forgot about it; by the time he returned, his syrup had reduced to a nice workable caramel that played nicely with the butterscotch notes in the tequila.

1 (1-inch) chunk poblano pepper, plus 1 slice for garnish

¾ ounce Pineapple "Caramel" (recipe follows)

2 ounces El Tesoro reposado tequila

½ ounce freshly squeezed lime juice

Pinch of salt

1 to 2 ounces carbonated water

Muddle the poblano and pineapple "caramel" in the bottom of a mixing glass. Add the tequila, lime juice, and salt and shake vigorously with ice to chill. Strain onto fresh ice in a rocks glass and top with a spritz of carbonated water. Garnish with the poblano slice.

PINEAPPLE "CARAMEL"

1 cup pineapple juice

1 cup sugar

Combine the ingredients in a medium-size saucepan over medium heat and bring to a simmer. Reduce until the consistency reaches that of a thin caramel.

ARTHUR WATSON'S BLOODY MARY

For nearly half a century, noted Texas interior designer Arthur Pope Watson lived with his partner, Bob Garrett, in a French-inspired mansion known only as the Chateau, perched on a bluff overlooking downtown Austin. Now in the shadow of the Frank Erwin Center, the house was built in the 1850s and was originally owned by the sister-in-law of James Bowie. Arthur and Bob played host to politicos, movie stars, and a who's who of Austin society—as famous as the priceless works of art were the cocktails, especially Arthur's Bloody Mary.

Before vodka gained prominence in the United States, there was a well-known cocktail called the Red Snapper, basically a gin Bloody Mary. Gordon's was the house gin at the Chateau. Chile pequins, also known as bird peppers for their propensity to sprout up under power lines, grow wildly around central Texas and were welcomed on the Chateau grounds. Muddling expresses the oil from these fiery peppers, giving this cocktail its memorable kick.

2 chile pequin peppers
½ teaspoon prepared horseradish
2 ounces gin
4 ounces tomato juice
½ ounce freshly squeezed lemon juice
¼ ounce Worcestershire sauce
2 dashes of Tabasco sauce
1 ounce beef consommé
½ teaspoon Sriracha
Sea salt and freshly ground black pepper
Pinch of celery salt
Lemon wedge, for garnish
Celery stick (with leaves), **for garnish**

In the bottom of a mixing glass, muddle the chile pequin peppers with the horseradish. Add all the remaining ingredients except the lemon and celery sticks, and fill the glass with ice. "Roll" the drink, pouring it a few times back and forth between another mixing glass or shaker tin to chill. (Shaking a Bloody Mary can yield a strangely unappealingly frothy drink.) Strain the contents onto fresh ice in a pint glass. Garnish with the lemon wedge and celery stick.

BLUE RIBBON

If you have members of your party who haven't yet warmed up to gin, this spring cocktail will change their minds. Hendrick's adds cucumber and rose to the typical botanical mix of London dry gin, making it perfectly suited for garden cocktails.

¼ cup blueberries

3 fresh basil leaves

4 fresh mint leaves

1 bar spoon Simple Syrup *(page 83)*

1½ ounces Hendrick's gin

½ ounce Luxardo maraschino liqueur

½ ounce freshly squeezed lime juice

Drop of lemon bitters

Lemon twist, for garnish

Muddle the blueberries, two of the basil leaves, and the mint and simple syrup in the bottom of a mixing glass. Add the gin, maraschino liqueur, lime juice, and bitters and shake vigorously with ice to chill. Fine-strain into a chilled cocktail glass. Garnish with the lemon twist and remaining basil leaf.

CAIPIRINHA

The national cocktail of Brazil, "Caipirinha" translates to something like "little country drink," like a hillbilly cousin to the Daiquiri. The Caipirinha is made with cachaça (pronounced ka-sha-sa), a rustic Brazilian cane spirit that is similar to *rhum agricole*. The drink's preparation is unique in a couple of ways. It is made by muddling the lime wedges, which releases not just the juice but also the essential oil from the skin and a small amount of bitterness from the pith. Additionally, it is one of the only drinks that is served with the ice with which it was shaken.

½ ounce Simple Syrup (page 83), or 1 heaping tablespoon superfine sugar (not powdered sugar)

1 lime, cut in half, core removed, sliced thinly (see picture)

2½ ounces cachaça

In the bottom of a mixing glass, muddle the simple syrup or sugar with the lime wedges. Add the cachaça and ice. Give the drink a quick shake of just a few seconds to chill; adjust the sweetness to your taste. Transfer the entire contents to a chilled rocks glass.

Technique Tip: Lime Wedges

It seems there are two primary schools of thought on how to cut a lime wedge. The first, most common method is what I call the Gringo Method. In the Gringo Method, the lime is cut in half longitudinally, and each hemisphere is cut into three or four wedges. (In a variation on the Gringo Method, the whole lime is cut in half along its equator, and then each north–south hemisphere is cut into quarters.) The other method I call the Mexican Method, in which the "faces" of the limes are cut away, leaving just the core behind. Both of these methods have their merits. The Gringo wedge makes for a lovely garnish when you cut a small notch in the "rib" and hang it on the rim of a glass. (This is also the preferred wedge shape for those who desire to suck on a lime wedge after shooting tequila. It should be noted that I, having graduated from college bars many years ago, do not fall into this camp. See Tequila, page 56.) The problem, however, is with that rib itself. In a lime, much of the fruit's bitterness resides in that rib that runs down the center. If you're going to be muddling lime wedges, as with a Caipirinha or Mojito, it might be better to follow the Mexican method—more juice and less pith. Regardless of what method you follow, it is almost always advised to wait until you need the lime wedge to cut it, as they don't store well. A dried-out, brown-around-the-edges lime wedge fails both at being squeezed and at beautifying a cocktail, though far too often this is the "garnish" we get, except in the more forward-thinking establishments.

GRINGO CUT

CANDELABRO

Pisco is a grape brandy, generally unaged, that is claimed by both Chile and Peru as their national spirit. Although best known as the base ingredient for the Pisco Sour cocktail, pisco is a versatile spirit that can be used in all manner of drinks. The name for this cocktail was not inspired by the flamboyant pianist Liberace, who was rarely without his candelabra; rather, by *El Candelabro*, an ancient petroglyph in the Peruvian Andes. You may need to adjust the amount of syrup depending on how sweet your cantaloupe is.

1½ ounces pisco

1½ ounces fresh-pressed cantaloupe juice *(or muddle ½ cup diced fresh cantaloupe in the glass before shaking)*

½ ounce freshly squeezed lime juice

Scant ½ ounce Simple Syrup *(page 83)*

½ ounce Cointreau or Paula's Texas Orange

Absinthe, for rinsing the glass

Cucumber wheel, for garnish

Combine the pisco, cantaloupe juice, lime juice, simple syrup, and Cointreau in a mixing glass with ice and shake vigorously to chill. Rinse a chilled cocktail glass with absinthe; strain the cocktail into the seasoned glass and garnish with the cucumber wheel.

CANTALOUPE

Texas cantaloupes are in their peak season right in the heat of summer. When they are ripe, they are juicy, sweet, and so fragrant you can smell ripe cantaloupe through their skin. Through the magic of modern agribusiness, cantaloupes are now available year-round, even if their flavor may suffer. A green or underripe cantaloupe will not be sweet and juicy for cocktail purposes, so sweetness must be adjusted to compensate.

For use in cocktails, cantaloupe can either be muddled or juiced. If you're making individual cocktails, muddling is the expeditious route. However, when making several or for a group, it is best to juice the fruit. A pulp extractor juicer is the easiest way to juice a cantaloupe. You may also use a blender: Trim and cut ripe cantaloupe and blend in a blender with the smallest amount of water necessary to keep the contents moving. Strain through a fine-mesh strainer to remove the pulp. Allow the juice to settle and strain off any foamy portion.

SONORA

Chris Bostick is a Texas bartender who cut his teeth at Austin's famous Fonda San Miguel restaurant before going west to ply his trade in Los Angeles. Back in Texas, one of his favorite cocktails is the Sonora. "I grew up eating cantaloupe with my grandfather, who'd crack fresh black pepper over it before we ate the fresh fruit," he explained. "And, of course, in Tex-Mexico a lot of people eat it with a squeeze of citrus and Mexican chile powders. Having grown up with it, cantaloupe to me is a quintessential part of summer refreshment here in central Texas."

½ cup chopped cantaloupe
½ ounce demerara syrup
2 ounces El Tesoro plata tequila
½ ounce Grand Marnier
1 ounce freshly squeezed lime juice
¼ teaspoon chile de arbol powder
Edible marigold, for garnish

In the bottom of a mixing glass, muddle the cantaloupe and demerara syrup. Add the tequila, Grand Marnier, lime juice, and chile de arbol powder and shake vigorously with ice to chill. Finely strain into a chilled coupe glass. Garnish with the edible marigold.

ORANGE LIQUEURS

You don't have to sleuth through too many cocktail recipes before the inevitable question arises of what the difference is between the various types of orange liqueurs. The categories are at best vague, though some characteristics are constant:

CURAÇAO

These liqueurs date back to the age of Dutch imperialism. The Dutch became proficient in producing a distillate flavored with dried orange peels from the Dutch Caribbean island of Curaçao. Curaçaos are usually brandy-based and may be blended with aged brandy or cognac and flavored with orange and other spices, such as vanilla, anise, and coriander. The product that most resembles historic curaçao comes from French cognac house Pierre Ferrand, which produces a brandy-based dry curaçao that is distilled with spices and orange peels and blended with aged cognac. Grand Marnier and Marie Brizard are prominent commercial brands. Curaçaos are best suited for cocktails made with aged spirits.

TRIPLE SEC

Good-quality triple sec is generally made from a neutral grain spirit or sugar beet distillate, as is the case with Cointreau, the most famous member of this category. There are nonalcoholic triple secs, which should be avoided. *Sec* means "dry," an odd descriptor for a liqueur, though in comparison to curaçao-style liqueurs, triple sec may seem lighter bodied and less sweet. Because the spirit is distilled after infusion, triple secs are clear in color and tend to have a pure orange flavor uncorrupted by other botanicals or aged spirits. Triple secs are great for citrus-based cocktails and cocktails made with unaged spirits.

PAULA'S TEXAS ORANGE

Paula's Texas Orange has been made in Austin since 2006 by Paula Angerstein, the first woman distiller in the state and owner of the second legal distillery in Texas (see page 42). It is made with a neutral grain base spirit that is macerated with fresh orange peels, then sweetened with cane sugar. It is more akin to an "orangecello" than a curaçao or triple sec, as the spirit is not redistilled after maceration. It has a very bright, clean orange flavor that works great in Margaritas and simple cocktails.

PAULA ANGERSTEIN

PAULA'S TEXAS SPIRITS

Paula Angerstein was born in Meyersville, a tiny town outside of the small town of Cuero in south Texas. After graduating from Cuero High, she left for the city and university life at UT Austin. Like many college students, she remained "undeclared" for as long as she could, "Limoncello Studies" not even crossing her mind at the time as a possible career path. Eventually she took a journalism class and a job at the *Daily Texan* and found her major. Angerstein said that, unfortunately, in the 1980s,

"I looked around and all of my journalism buddies who'd graduated were out of work. So I decided to double-major in computer science."

The summer after graduation, Angerstein spent the best six hundred dollars of her life and embarked on a fifty-five-day European adventure, on a group tour that took her all over the continent. When she later returned to the States, her decision to double-major would be fortuitous and provided the perfect skill set for a job in the field of technical writing. Eventually she got into programming, and her career in the software field took her to Southern California, and, of course, back to

Europe. In the late 1980s she began traveling abroad regularly for work, first to Hamburg and Paris, and eventually to Windsor, England, where she lived for a couple of years in the early 1990s. It was during this time that she fell in love with Paul, who has been her partner in crime ever since. Together they fell in love with Italy, when a last-minute villa reservation in Tuscany led to a magical week during the running of the famous Il Palio race in Sienna.

They were so enamored of Tuscany that they vowed to return every year for the rest of their lives—a promise they have kept to this day, with only a few exceptions. Angerstein is quick to point out that she has not always been dialed in to the food of the Italian kitchen. "I was sixteen the first time I had pizza," she reminisced, "and that was when Pizza Hut came to Cuero."

So how did a programmer with a love of Europe become the first female distiller in Texas? "We learned about limoncello during our trips to Italy," Angerstein recalled. "Then years later, my sister gave me a recipe she found in a magazine for how to make it at home. We originally just did it for ourselves and for friends and family." When Angerstein decided she wanted to make limoncello professionally, she got a friendly word of advice that changed the course of her business. "At the advice of Russell Smith, we decided to make orange liqueur first. Texas is a Margarita market, and you can't make a Margarita without a good orange liqueur." In February 2005, Angerstein released Paula's Texas Orange, the first orange liqueur to be made in Texas. In October 2006, she followed that up with Paula's Texas Lemon. The timing couldn't have been better, as Angerstein launched at the beginning of what would become a deluge of local spirits and an appreciation for local products in general.

While Angerstein is known professionally as the first lady of Texas spirits, she is known personally as the consummate hostess. The parties at Paul and Paula's house are legendary, to be sure, but a weeknight dinner for them is no less impressive. She traces her hospitality skills back to the "good standard country living" of her childhood. "The Lutheran Church potlucks were the big show. Everybody brought specialties that they were famous for—the bar was pretty high. Women served wine rice and black-eyed peas, while the men smoked brisket." Whatever the occasion, Angerstein is certain to make sure there is no shortage of refreshments. "Our favorite way to enjoy Paula's Texas Orange is in the Paula's Margarita. And Paula's Lemon, pulled straight from the freezer, is a great way to cap off a summer meal." 🌿

CORPSE REVIVER 3000

Corpse Revivers were once a category of drinks, what might now be categorized as "hair of the dog" cocktails. The most famous of these is the Corpse Reviver No. 2, of which Harry Craddock wrote in his 1930 *Savoy Cocktail Book*, "Four of these taken in quick succession will unrevive the corpse again." By the end of the twentieth century, No. 2 was the only Corpse Reviver anyone could remember, if in fact they knew any at all. In this variation on No. 2, absinthe replaces the gin, and St-Germain fills in for Lillet—a Corpse Reviver of the future.

¾ **ounce Tenneyson Absinthe Royale or other blanche absinthe**

¾ **ounce St-Germain elderflower liqueur**

¾ **ounce orange liqueur** *(we used Paula's Texas Orange; Cointreau also works well)*

¾ **ounce freshly squeezed lemon juice**

Orange "coin," for garnish

Combine the absinthe, St-Germain, orange liqueur, and lemon juice in a mixing glass and shake vigorously with ice to chill. Strain into a chilled cocktail glass and garnish with the orange "coin."

ABSINTHE

In the history of spirits, the chapter on absinthe is perhaps the most mystifying. In the span of about two hundred years, absinthe went from relative obscurity to muse of the belle epoque to scapegoat for the ills of industrialization. Demonized, banned, fetishized, and re-legalized—what is all the fuss about?

Absinthe takes its name from *Artemesia absinthium*, the scientific name for grand wormwood. Wormwood has been used since ancient times for its purported anthelmintic qualities. Wormwood, anise, and fennel are the core botanicals in absinthe, which emerged in the late eighteenth century around the small Swiss village of Couvet, near the French-Swiss border. Like many herbal spirits, absinthe has its roots in the early European apothecary tradition of distilling plants—roots, stems, herbs, flowers, barks, and so on— in alcohol for their purported pharmacological benefits.

Absinthe gained popularity in the early part of the nineteenth century, with no small thanks to the French military, which issued it as an antimalarial to soldiers fighting abroad. Absinthe got another boost when the French wine industry was devastated by the grapevine pest *Phylloxera* in the 1860s and '70s. With cheap wine temporarily unavailable, drinkers turned to other sources for spirited amusement, and no small number of them turned to absinthe. Absinthe was particularly popular amongst the writers and artists of the belle epoque, and figures prominently in paintings by Degas, Picasso, Van Gogh, and others.

The wine industry was none too pleased with this development, and when the vineyards recovered, the industry launched a campaign to reclaim sales lost to absinthe drinkers. The temperance movement that was afoot on American shores would never have been capable of banning all alcohol from French commerce because wine production in that country is deeply imbedded in their cultural heritage. But it found a willing partner in the wine producers, and together they were able to create a distinction: Wine was natural, agricultural, traditional, and healthful. Absinthe, on the other hand, was industrial, foreign, newfangled, and toxic.

The case against absinthe was assisted by some junk science of the period: Wormwood contains the component thujone, which was rumored to have psychoactive or other deleterious properties. Physicians conjured up the "disease" absinthism, which was more likely just good old-fashioned alcoholism dressed up for political purposes. A series of unfortunately timed, sensationalist "absinthe murders" drove the final nail into absinthe's coffin. The Swiss were the first to ban absinthe in 1910, the Americans followed suit in 1912, and finally the French closed the books on absinthe in 1914. Tried for a crime it did not commit and found guilty in the court of public opinion, absinthe was outlawed in just about any place it had been relevant.

If not for the efforts of a few absinthe evangelists such as Ted Breaux, absinthe might have stayed forever in history's dustbin. But the efforts of Breaux and others paid off, as they proved that absinthe was not dangerous to your health—at least not more so than any other alcoholic beverage. The long-standing ban was lifted, and finally in 2007, authentic French absinthe was imported again to the United States for the first time in almost a century.

ABSINTHE USE

The classic way absinthe would have been enjoyed in the belle epoque was in a traditional drip: About 1 ounce of spirit is poured into an absinthe or "Pontarlier" glass. If sugar is desired, a perforated spoon is placed across the mouth of the glass, and a sugar cube is placed on the spoon. Water is slowly dripped or poured over the sugar cube, which dissolves (with high-quality modern absinthes, sugar is not necessary unless preferred by the drinker).

As the water content rises in the glass, the absinthe undergoes a visual change from transparent green to opaque jade, in what is known as a louche (pronounced "loosh"). The louche effect is caused by essential oils from the distilled herbs (specifically a substance known as trans-anethol, present in all anise-flavored spirits) that are soluble in alcohol but insoluble in water. As water is added to the glass, the alcohol concentration decreases, and anethol precipitates out of the solution, thus giving the appearance of clouding the liquid. Although absinthe is the most notorious of the spirits that louche, it is not the only one: All manner of anise and herbal spirits found around the Mediterranean will undergo the process, some more subtly than others.

There is much ritual associated with the absinthe drip and while I myself enjoy all the accoutrements, you do not need to amass a collection of absinthe-specific gear to enjoy absinthe. At its most basic, you only need some kind of glass to drink it from, and some kind of vessel to pour iced water from.

Before absinthe's ban, it was a well-known cocktail ingredient, though frequently it was used only in dashes, drops, and rinses—more of a cocktail seasoning than the main show. The Sazerac (page 176) is the most famous of these, though at this point in time, the Sazerac has been made with Herbsaint, an anise liqueur, for more of its history than it has been with authentic absinthe. You will find a number of recipes in this book that feature absinthe as either the main spirit or best supporting actor. Specifically, I have used Tenneyson, a *blanche* absinthe made at the historic Emile Pernot distillery in Pontarlier, France, for an Austin-based spirits company. Tenneyson utilizes traditional absinthe herbs but also incorporates typical gin botanicals such as juniper and lemon peel. It's gin-reminiscent profile and comparatively low proof (106 proof, or 53 percent alcohol by volume) make it a perfect spirit for mixing cocktails.

ABSINTHE STYLES

Verte absinthes, true to their name, are green in color. Like all distilled spirits, absinthe comes off the still clear. *Verte* absinthes undergo a secondary herbal infusion that gives absinthe its famous color.

Blanche absinthes are clear out of the bottle, and become white when they are louched. This style is common of Swiss absinthe, and is sometimes known as *la bleue*, especially when the absinthe is made clandestinely, as much of it was in absinthe's heartland during absinthe's almost century-long ban in Switzerland.

"Bohemian" is the euphemism used to describe absinthes that deemphasize the anise profile and are generally cold-compounded with essences dissolved in high-proof alcohol. This typifies the no-*e* "abinsths" that started coming out of the Czech Republic (where absinthe was never banned), the most famous of which was the Hill's brand. Bohemian absinthes played an important role in renewing interest in absinthe, though, unfortunately, they tend to lack the nuance and elegance of traditional distilled absinthe. 🍸

DAIQUIRI

The Daiquiri is one of the great, misunderstood classic cocktails.
Its original formula is almost impossibly simple: rum, lime, and sugar.
It was created in late-nineteenth-century Cuba in the days shortly after
the Spanish-American War and gained popularity in the bars of Havana
before traveling, according to legend, to Washington DC's Army and Navy
Club via Admiral Lucius Johnson. The versions found in the "Daiquiri shacks"
of America's beach towns, chain restaurants, and college towns, and on
the streets of New Orleans bear little resemblance to the elegant Cuban
classic. Forget Daiquiri "mixes." All you need are a few limes, some sugar
(preferably a raw type, but the white stuff works), and good rum. The classic
Daiquiri would have been made with dry white rum, but the drink is also
fabulous with your favorite aged rum or with a *rhum agricole*.

2 ounces white rum
1 ounce freshly squeezed lime juice
1 ounce Simple Syrup *(page 83)*
Lime wheel, for garnish

Combine the rum, lime juice, and simple
syrup in a mixing glass and shake vigorously
with ice to chill. Adjust the amount of syrup
to taste. Strain into a chilled cocktail glass.
Garnish with the lime wheel.

FIG DAIQUIRI

There is a sexiness to figs that borders on the obscene; no wonder their leaves were used by censors of ancient art to cover, ahem, objectionable parts. Figs grow especially well in central Texas, if you can keep them away from the squirrels and other critters long enough to let them ripen for picking. The taste of fresh figs when you eat them raw is not just fruity, but also earthy, vegetal, and primordial. When used in cocktails, their sweetness comes forward—any number of classic cocktails can benefit from the addition of a few ripe figs.

---

4 small or 2 large ripe figs, stems removed, cut in half, plus 1 whole fig for garnish

¾ ounce Simple Syrup *(page 83)*

2 ounces white rum

1 ounce freshly squeezed lime juice

In the bottom of a mixing glass, muddle the halved figs and simple syrup. Add the rum and lime juice and shake vigorously with ice to chill. Adjust the amount of syrup to taste. Fine-strain into a chilled cocktail glass. Garnish with the whole fig.

AGRICOLE DAIQUIRI WITH FRESH PEACH

The Daiquiri is such a simple cocktail, it serves as a great platform for experimentation. Changing around the base spirit and source of sweetness can result in some surprisingly delicious variations. Here *rhum agricole* (below) replaces molasses rum, and its visceral, vegetal qualities play nicely with sweet-tart peaches.

1 small or ½ large ripe peach, diced, plus 1 peach slice for garnish

¾ ounce Simple Syrup *(page 83)*

2 ounces rhum agricole

4 drops Bitter Truth Jerry Thomas's Own Decanter Bitters

¾ ounce freshly squeezed lime juice

In the bottom of a mixing glass, muddle the peach and simple syrup. You may need to adjust the amount of syrup depending upon how sweet your peach is. Add the *rhum agricole*, bitters, and lime juice and shake vigorously with ice to chill. Fine-strain into a chilled cocktail glass. Garnish with the peach slice.

RHUM AGRICOLE

From the French islands in the West Indies, specifically Martinique, comes a unique style of rum known as *rhum agricole*. Whereas most rum is made from molasses, a by-product of the sugar-refining process, *rhum agricole* is made from fresh-pressed sugarcane juice, harvested locally to the distillery. The resulting spirit is earthy, grassy, vegetal, and herbaceous—not to mention pricey. The quality of Martinique *rhum* is assured by the French government through an Appellation d'Origine Contrôlée (AOC), or a protected appellation of origin, for *rhums* that meet certain standards of production. As a result, AOC Rhum Martinique must adhere to standards of production and consistency as rigorous as those for other AOC products, such as Cognac, Armagnac, and Champagne.

EL PEPINO

There is an unfortunate tendency to pigeonhole any tequila drink as being some kind of Margarita—just take a look at the menu at your favorite Tex-Mex restaurant, and there may be a dozen Margarita variations on the menu. In reality, tequila is a versatile spirit and deserves to be recognized beyond its (considerable) contribution to the Margarita. On a hot day you'd be hard pressed to find a cocktail more refreshing than this combination of tequila, cool mint, and cucumber.

⅓ cup fresh diced cucumber
1 ounce Mint Syrup *(recipe follows)*
2 ounces 100% agave silver tequila
½ ounce freshly squeezed lime juice
Fresh mint, for garnish
Cucumber spear, for garnish
Mezcal *(optional)*

In the bottom of a mixing glass, muddle the cucumber and mint syrup. Add the tequila and lime juice and shake vigorously with ice to chill. Strain into a double Old Fashioned glass filled with crushed ice. Garnish abundantly with fresh mint and a cucumber spear.
Optional: Float a small amount of mezcal on top of the cocktail to add a smoky aroma.

MINT SYRUP

1 cup raw sugar
or evaporated cane juice
1 cup filtered water
1 cup packed fresh mint leaves

In a saucepan, bring the sugar and water to a simmer. Add the mint and allow it to infuse until a prominent mint flavor develops, about 10 minutes. Strain out the mint and allow the syrup to cool. Store refrigerated for up to 1 month.

TEQUILA

...s is one of the largest markets for tequila consumption in the United
...es. Texans practically grow up drinking the stuff and have a special love
...not just with tequila, but with its homeland as well. It is as if tequila
...bolizes a carefree life—however far-fetched—that we imagine in "old"
...co. But this bonhomie belies the much more complex reality of tequila
...uction—the social, agricultural, ecological, and economic implications
...nd the beverage with which we lubricate our memories.

...quila starts with the Weber Blue agave. A member of the lily family,
...er Blue is one of hundreds of agaves that grow in Mexico, but the only
...allowed in tequila production. After as much as six to a dozen or more
...s in the ground, the plants are harvested by trimming off the outer
...es, the *pencas*. What is left is the *piña*, so named for its resemblance to
...mmed pineapple. *Piñas* are transported to the distillery, where they
...oasted in clay brick ovens. Once roasted, agaves are crushed and the
...s washed with water to yield *aguamiel* (honey-water). Yeast is added to
...combination of water and agave sugars to start fermentation, whereby
...hes are converted to alcohol. The fermented *mosto* makes its way to
...till, where it will pass through two times (tequila is distilled at least two
...s by law, sometimes more). The first distillation results in low-proof
...*ario*; after the liquid is distilled the second time, it is known as tequila

All tequila, by definition, must be distilled in Mexico from agaves that are grown in the five-state area that comprises the Denominación de Origen de Tequila. Tequila falls into two primary categories. The first, and finest, is 100% agave, which means that all of the sugar is from agave only, and that the tequila must be bottled in Mexico. Most 100% agave tequila is sold unaged and is identified as *plata*, or silver (*plata* tequilas can be aged for up to two months in wood, though most are not). Tequila that is aged for two to twelve months in oak barrels is called *reposado* (rested), and when it is aged for one to two years, it is known as *añejo*. There is a newer category of tequilas called *extra-añejo*—these are aged for more than two years.

The larger category is what we call *mixto* (known in Mexico as *tequila regular*), which means it is a blend of sugars from agave and other sources, such as cane and grain. So-called gold tequila is unaged *mixto* tequila that is also known as *joven abocado* (young and smoothed). Generally a tequila is "smoothed" by age in an oak barrel, but gold tequila comes by its smoothness with the addition of caramel and other flavorings, which give it the appearance and sensation of having been aged.

Mixto tequila by law must contain only a minimum of 51 percent agave sugar and can be sold in bulk and bottled in other countries.

Tequila consumption has soared in recent years, and with that demand comes a number of challenges. Because agaves take many years to mature—as much as eight to ten years is not uncommon—it is difficult to predict what tequila consumption is going to be like by the time the agaves are ready to be harvested. So the farmers basically have to guess on the amount they plant.

Agaves are propagated from little offshoots called *hijuelos* that are genetic clones of the parents. The plants don't cross-pollinate, which weakens them against diseases and pests. The more profound threat to traditional tequila has to do with changes to the production process. Technological advances can increase yield by as much as 3 percent; however, they can also be used to incorporate chemicals into a once organic process. The popularity of tequila has also led to multinational corporations scooping up distilleries. As facilities industrialize, the resulting tequilas can change, becoming less traditional, lighter, less vegetal, and, in a way, less tequila-y. ♣

FACUNDO'S FIX

I made this cocktail for the Bacardi Legacy competition. My goal was to create a cocktail in the mold of the great Bacardi "legacy" drinks such as the Daiquiri and the Mojito.

1½ ounces Bacardi Superior rum

¾ ounce freshly squeezed lemon juice

¾ ounce Benedictine

1 bar spoon Simple Syrup (page 83)

Flamed lemon peel, for garnish

Combine the rum, lemon juice, Benedictine, and simple syrup in a mixing glass with ice and shake vigorously to chill. Strain into a chilled cocktail glass and garnish with the flamed lemon peel.

FLOR DE PIÑA

Most people think of tiki and immediately think of rum. But tiki-era cocktails were as diverse as the bartenders who made them. As long as they captured the essence of the tropics, tiki drinks could be made with anything from gin to brandy to absinthe. We honor that tradition here with this tequila tiki drink.

1½ ounces 100% agave silver tequila

¾ ounce St-Germain elderflower liqueur

1 ounce pineapple juice

½ ounce freshly squeezed lime juice

½ ounce Canela Syrup (page 59)

Pineapple wedge, for garnish

Combine the tequila, elderflower liqueur, pineapple juice, lime juice, and *canela* syrup in a mixing glass and shake vigorously with ice to chill. Strain into a tiki mug filled with crushed ice. Garnish with the pineapple wedge.

CANELA SYRUP

1 cup raw sugar, processed sugar, or evaporated cane juice

1 cup filtered water

2 large Mexican-style cinnamon sticks (*sold as* canela *in the Mexican grocery section*)

In a saucepan, bring the sugar and water to a simmer. Break up the cinnamon sticks and add to the pan; allow to infuse until a prominent cinnamon flavor develops, about 15 minutes. Strain out the cinnamon sticks and allow the syrup to cool. Store refrigerated for up to 1 month.

GIMLET

The Gimlet holds a special place in my heart, as it was one of the first grown-up drinks I ever learned to order, once I was old enough and had the sensibility to drink in establishments that utilized vessels other than disposable plastic cups. Unfortunately, as I learned more about the role of fresh and natural ingredients in cocktails, the Gimlet's appeal began to wane, due to the problematic nature of one of its two ingredients: Rose's Lime Juice. Rose's began its life in the late nineteenth century as a "lime cordial"—lime juice preserved with enough sugar to keep it fresh, especially across long ocean voyages. A century later, however, the famous cordial had lost much of its luster, and the modern version available in the United States contains artificial colors and artificial flavors, and is sweetened with high-fructose corn syrup (in other countries it may still be made with cane sugar). Some bartenders responded by making Gimlets with fresh lime juice and sugar; whereas this combination might make a perfectly delightful tipple, a Gimlet it is not. By tradition and by definition, the Gimlet is made with *preserved* lime juice. The answer to this drinker's dilemma is to make your own lime cordial, which has much more complexity than the simple marriage of lime juice and sugar, and will give new life to this turn-of-the-century classic. Although traditionally made with gin, the Gimlet is also often made with vodka, too.

2½ ounces gin

2 ounces house-made Lime Cordial
(page 62)

Lime wheel, for garnish

Combine the gin and lime cordial in a mixing glass. Shake vigorously with ice to chill, then strain into a chilled cocktail glass. Garnish with the lime wheel.

LIME CORDIAL

Makes about 2½ cups

1 dozen medium-size ripe Persian limes

About 1½ cups sugar

Wash the limes in warm water to remove the produce wax. Allow to dry.

Place the 1½ cups sugar in a mixing bowl. Using a vegetable peeler, carefully remove the very outermost zest from the limes, taking off as little pith as possible. As you remove the zest, make sure that the action is directed over the bowl, so that the sugar may absorb as much expressed oil as possible. It is, after all, the essential oil in the skin that is the lime's most prized

possession. After all of the zest has been added to the sugar, use a muddler to gently press the zest into the sugar; the abrasion will allow the essential oil in the zest to be released into the sugar. Set aside and allow to infuse for about 30 minutes.

Meanwhile, cut the limes in half and juice them, taking care to strain through a fine-mesh strainer. Measure the lime juice and add enough sugar to the bowl so that the amount of sugar by volume is equal to the amount of lime juice by volume (e.g., if there are 2 cups of lime juice, add ½ cup of sugar to the existing amount in the bowl). Add the lime juice to the sugar and stir continuously until all the sugar is dissolved, leaving the lime zest in the syrup. Cover and store in the refrigerator. After 6 to 8 hours, taste the cordial. If it is to your liking, strain out the lime zest and bottle. For more complex flavor, leave the zest in overnight. Store refrigerated for up to 1 month.

HOT SUMMER NIGHT

In 2007, Houston native Mindy Kucan won an international cocktail competition amongst Hilton Hotels bartenders with this cocktail. Her accomplishment helped put Texas bartenders on the map in those early days of the craft cocktail revival in these parts. At the urging of legendary barman Tony Abou-Ganim, and with the help of an eager group of bartenders, in 2008 she founded the Austin chapter of the United States Bartenders Guild, the first chapter in Texas.

¾ ounce Honey Syrup *(recipe follows)*

2 sprigs fresh thyme

¾ ounce freshly squeezed lemon juice

1½ ounces Tito's Handmade Vodka

½ ounce Paula's Texas Lemon *(or limoncello if you are outside Texas)*

1 ounce natural lemon or lemon-lime soda

Lemon wheel, for garnish

Combine the honey syrup, one thyme sprig, and the lemon juice, vodka, and Paula's Texas Lemon in a mixing glass and shake vigorously with ice to chill. Fine-strain into a Collins glass with fresh ice. Top with the lemon soda and garnish with the second thyme sprig and the lemon wheel.

HONEY SYRUP

Honey is a fabulous cocktail ingredient and dates to ancient times as a sweetener for beverages. Unfortunately, you can't use honey as-is, straight out of the jar, as ice and honey don't mix. Instead, make a syrup of equal parts hot water and honey. It will not only pour more easily than straight honey, it will also dissolve more readily into your cocktail. Store it covered in the refrigerator for up to two weeks.

GOLDEN GATE SWIZZLE

This cocktail comes from Houston bartender Matt Tanner. Although it contains a full ounce and a half of Fernet Branca, the heady Italian *amaro* (digestif), this cocktail was made to be a refreshing introduction to that sometimes-polarizing spirit. Its name pays homage to San Francisco, which is known to be one of the largest per-capita consumers of Fernet Branca in the world.

1½ ounces Fernet Branca
1 ounce freshly squeezed lemon juice
¾ ounce Orgeat *(page 109)*
¼ ounce Taylor's Velvet Falernum
6 dashes of Angostura orange bitters
4 dashes of Angostura aromatic bitters
Large fresh mint sprig, for garnish
Orange slice, for garnish

Build the liquid ingredients in a Collins glass filled with crushed ice. Using a swizzle stick or a bar spoon, "swizzle" the drink by rubbing the stick or spoon in the palm of your hand back and forth as the drink chills and the glass frosts. Garnish with a generous bouquet of mint and the orange slice.

LA MARIQUITA

I am generally not a fan of the flavored vodkas, preferring instead to use fresh ingredients to achieve the desired result. There are a few exceptions to this rule. Graham's Texas Tea is made in Austin by Treaty Oak Distilling, naturally flavored by steeping Nilgiri black tea and sweetened with cane sugar.

2 ounces Graham's Texas Tea
1 ounce St-Germain elderflower liqueur
¾ ounce freshly squeezed lemon juice
2 ounces carbonated water
Lemon wheel, for garnish

Combine the Graham's Texas Tea, elderflower liqueur, and lemon juice in a mixing glass with ice and shake vigorously to chill. Strain into a Collins glass filled with fresh ice. Top with the carbonated water and garnish with the lemon wheel.

LOVE BITE ⚲

The very thought of a "Valentine's Day cocktail" makes me shudder in fear of attempting to re-create the flavor of a chocolate-covered cherry in liquid form—all done up in holiday drag with chocolate shavings and sprinkles, as that is the typical mold for such drinks. I took the opposite approach here, with a cocktail for those whose idea of romance involves just a little nibble.

1½ ounces Tito's Handmade Vodka

½ ounce Tenneyson Absinthe Royale or other blanche absinthe

½ ounce raspberry syrup, such as Monin or another coffee shop brand *(or muddle fresh raspberries with a touch of Simple Syrup, page 83)*

¾ ounce pineapple juice

½ ounce freshly squeezed lime juice

1 raspberry, for garnish

Combine all the ingredients except the raspberry in a mixing glass and shake vigorously with ice to chill. Strain into a chilled cocktail glass and garnish with the raspberry.

MATAGALPA ⚲

Essentially an aged-rum Margarita, this cocktail was originally made with eighteen-year-old Flor de Caña rum, but tastes great with any number of aged rums.

1½ ounces Flor de Caña Centenario Gold eighteen-year-old rum

¾ ounce Cointreau or Paula's Texas Orange

½ ounce freshly squeezed lime juice

½ ounce Simple Syrup *(page 83)*

Flamed orange peel, for garnish

Combine the rum, Cointreau, lime juice, and simple syrup in a mixing glass with ice; shake vigorously to chill. Strain into a chilled cocktail glass and garnish with the flamed orange peel.

LOVE BITE

HOW TO DRINK FLUENT MEXICAN

WITH CLAUDIA ALARCÓN

I decided to reach out to my friend and colleague Claudia Alarcón, a veteran figure in Austin's food and beverage journalism scene, with a few questions about Mexican and Mexican-style drinks. Alarcón hails from Mexico City but has called Austin her home since the 1980s. I had a burning question about Margarita service in Mexico. In Texas, two standard questions are almost certain to follow when you order a Margarita in a restaurant, and in many bars: Would you like that on the rocks or frozen? Would you like salt or no salt? Most Margarita drinkers are familiar enough with the routine that they preempt the question. But I take issue with the question itself. It seems like the proper question would be to ask if the drinker preferred the drink straight up or on the rocks. Where did the frozen version come from?

"In Mexico, a frozen Margarita was unheard of until fairly recently," Alarcón said by way of confirming my suspicion. "But now they're popular in places like Mexico City because of international chain restaurants like TGI Friday's—so the frozen Margarita was imported to Mexico from the United States. Because it's from the States, it's a novelty." Traditionally it would have been served shaken and served up into a V-shaped stemmed glass, which brings me to my next Margarita conundrum: the Mexican Martini.

"By the early 1980s, the Margarita was ubiquitous in Texas, but it wasn't necessarily good or made correctly," Alarcón explained. "It turns out most places used a Margarita mix, with varying degrees of artificiality, so the folks at the Cedar Door started serving what they called a Mexican Margarita: Tequila, Cointreau, and lime juice, shaken and strained into a stemmed glass. It was a traditional Margarita, served traditionally. Unfortunately, the revival wouldn't last forever."

"Over time, Austinites started calling the Mexican Margarita the Mexican Martini, because of the stemmed glass. Eventually, the bartenders started serving the shaker on the side, and now we're at the current situation with the Mexican Martini," Alarcón told me. And the current situation is a far cry from that early attempt at bringing back the traditional Margarita. My research into the Mexican Martini at several prominent bars, two of which claim to have invented it, revealed widespread use of a number of ingredients that have no place in a Margarita, such as orange juice, olive juice, Margarita mix, and Sprite. At its best, a Mexican Martini is really just a classic top-shelf Margarita, served in a stemmed glass (with an olive garnish if you feel so compelled).

All of this talk of Margaritas obscures the fact that the drink is far more popular in the United States than in Mexico. According to Alarcón, if Mexicans are going to drink tequila, it is more likely to be in a Paloma, or served neat with a side of Sangrita. Not to be confused with Sangria, Sangrita (meaning "little blood") is a mixture of juice and spice that is served as an accompaniment to tequila. Although the number of recipes is virtually infinite, two differing schools of thought prevail: the pomegranate school and the tomato school. The pomegranate school seems to be the more traditional, in which Sangrita is made from a mix of orange and lime juices with grenadine and spices. The tomato school recipe derives its red color from tomato as opposed to pomegranate and chiles. Either way, the Sangrita is taken in small sips between sips of 100% agave tequila and acts as a little palate cleanser and palate stimulant. "In reality, tequila isn't the main thing people drink in Mexico. Scotch, rum, brandy, and Coke are all very common," Alarcón said, "and no shortage of beer and Micheladas."

CLAUDIA ALARCÓN'S SANGRITA

This recipe is easy to make and is nicely balanced between sweet and savory, spicy and tart. Of course, you can adjust the spice to your liking. *Makes about 4 cups*

¼ medium-size white onion

2 cups freshly squeezed orange juice

2 cups tomato juice or Clamato juice

½ cup freshly squeezed lime juice

2 tablespoons house-made or natural grenadine

¼ cup hot sauce (such as *Valentina)*, or to taste

1 teaspoon salt

Using a fine grater, grate the onion over a bowl fitted with a fine-mesh strainer. Discard the pulpy part. In a pitcher, combine the onion juice with the remaining ingredients. Stir thoroughly and chill.

PALOMA

The Paloma is the second-most-famous tequila cocktail after the Margarita, but it is number one as consumed in Mexico. You can make it with grapefruit juice and club soda, but it is more traditionally made with a grapefruit soda such as Squirt.

2 ounces 100% agave tequila

½ ounce freshly squeezed lime juice

Pinch of kosher salt

3 ounces grapefruit soda

Lime wedge, for garnish

Build all the ingredients, except the lime wedge, over ice in a Collins glass and stir gently to combine. Garnish with the lime wedge.

MICHELADA

The thing that rears its head in contemporary bars as a "Michelada" bears little resemblance to the drink as it is known in Mexico—a simple, perfectly refreshing concoction of beer and lime served on the rocks in a salted glass. This is quite spartan by today's standards, when a Michelada is likely to come with an assortment of accompaniments that look as if they escaped from the Bloody Mary cart. As Claudia Alarcón explains it, Bloody Mary mix is a latter-day gringo additive: "Somewhere along the way it got corrupted." A shot of mezcal or tequila on the side, however, is perfectly traditional.

Salt	First, salt the rim of a pint glass, if that is
1 ounce freshly squeezed lime juice	your preference. Fill the glass with ice and
1 (12-ounce) can or bottle Mexican beer	add the lime juice. Pour in the beer.

BARRO NEGRO

If the Margarita and Paloma are the "official" drinks of tequila, what is the official drink of mezcal? This is my nomination, a mezcal version of a Cuba Libre. Barro Negro is a distinct type of black pottery unique to Oaxaca, the homeland of mezcal.

1½ ounces mezcal
2 dashes of Angostura bitters
2 orange wedges
3 ounces Mexican Coca-Cola

Add the mezcal and bitters to an ice-filled Old Fashioned glass. Squeeze in the juice of the orange wedges and drop the wedges into the glass. Top with the Mexican Coca-Cola and give it a stir.

MEXICAN COCA-COLA

Coca-Cola is made with slight variations wherever in the world it is made. In Mexico, many of the bottling plants still use cane sugar to sweeten the soda, as opposed to high-fructose corn syrup (because of government corn subsidies in the United States, it is cheaper for manufacturers to use corn syrup instead of cane sugar, and so most sodas are bottled accordingly). Much Mexican Coke is still bottled in glass bottles with the painted label. Whether it's for nostalgia reasons or perceived health benefits, Texans have long had a love affair with Mexican Coke, and it can be found on the ethnic specialty or specialty soda shelf of many grocery stores.

MARGARITA

As far as cocktails-ordered-by-name go, the Margarita is one of the most popular drinks in the United States, and it has been a staple in Texas and the Southwest for decades. Many creation myths obscure the origin of the Margarita, though the most likely scenario is that it is a Tequila variation on the Daisy. Daisies were a pre-Prohibition category of cocktails consisting of a base spirit, citrus, and a flavored sweetener—such as curaçao.

For many years, artificially enhanced "gold" tequila was the most common variety available. Recent years have changed that, and there are dozens of high-quality tequilas on the market. To make the best Margarita, use only 100% agave tequilas, freshly squeezed lime juice, and a good-quality orange liqueur.

---

2 ounces 100% agave silver tequila

¾ ounce Cointreau or Paula's Texas Orange

¾ ounce freshly squeezed lime juice

1 bar spoon Simple Syrup (page 83; optional, for those who prefer a sweeter cocktail)

Kosher salt (optional)

Lime wedge, for garnish

Combine the tequila, orange liqueur, lime juice, and simple syrup with ice in a cocktail shaker. Shake vigorously with the ice to properly chill and emulsify the ingredients. Strain into a salt-rimmed, chilled cocktail glass or onto fresh ice in a rocks glass or footed goblet. Garnish with the lime wedge.

A Note on the Skinny Margarita: *The so-called skinny Margarita phenomenon has gained traction in recent years, much to the chagrin of traditionalists like myself. If you look at it rationally, booze has calories, and there's no way of getting around those calories if you're a person who likes to drink. Ethyl alcohol contributes most of the calories to the cocktails we drink, when we drink a traditional cocktail. What is not skinny is the added, and in my opinion unnecessary, calories in mixes. So if you drink a traditional Margarita, made only with tequila, lime, and a little bit of orange liqueur, the drink has about the same calories as the bottled product from the reality TV star and tastes a whole lot better.*

PERSIMMON MARGARITA

Persimmons are one of the hallmarks of fall. From the time the temperature drops until the holidays, persimmons start making their way to the local farmers' market. The waiting game can be almost unbearable, but once they are finally ripe, the reward justifies the wait. My favorite thing to do with persimmons is to press the ultra-ripe fruit through a fine-mesh strainer, discard the skin and seeds, and shake the resulting pulp into my fall Margaritas.

2 ounces reposado tequila

2 ounces Paula's Texas Orange

2 ounces persimmon puree

1 ounce freshly squeezed lime juice

Cinnamon-Sugar-Cayenne rim
(see Abbeville Daiquiri, page 131)

Combine all the liquid ingredients in a mixing glass and shake vigorously with ice to chill and emulsify. Strain onto fresh ice in a pint glass rimmed with cinnamon-sugar-cayenne rim.

PERSIMMONS

There is a variety of persimmon native to Texas that is small and turns black when ripe. However, I recommend using fuyu persimmons, which are sweet even when hard, and turn to a sweet, supple, mixable pudding.

Gently wash the soft, ripe persimmons and remove the stems and the leaves at the top. Using a rubber spatula, press the persimmons through a fine-mesh strainer set over a mixing bowl. Scrape the outside of the strainer to make sure you get any clinging pulp, and discard the skin and seeds. The strained persimmons yield a pudding-like puree that can be used for cocktails and baking. It can be kept covered in the refrigerator for up to 1 week.

FROZEN MARGARITA

This is it—the Tipsy Tasting Panel has devoted hours and days to rigorous research so that you can enjoy the best possible Margarita in frozen form. Gone are the days of canned, bottled, or powdered mixes. This easy-to-make recipe will forever convert you to the timeless charm of the fresh lime frozen Margarita. While this may seem like a lot of booze (and it is), this recipe is sized to fit the typical blown-glass Margarita stemware common to many Tex-Mex restaurants. Realistically, it could be two reasonably sized Margaritas.

2 ounces 100% agave tequila

**2 ounces Cointreau
or Paula's Texas Orange**

2½ ounces freshly squeezed lime juice

1 ounce Simple Syrup *(page 83)*

Coarse salt *(optional)*

Lime wedge, for garnish

Combine the tequila, Cointreau, lime juice, and simple syrup in a blender cup and fill with ice until the ice is just covered by the liquid. Blend thoroughly (it may be necessary to add a little bit more ice to achieve the desired slushiness). Pour into a goblet, rimmed with coarse salt if you like, and garnish with the lime wedge.

Note: *For a Frozen Margarita à la San Antonio, upend a bottle of Big Red into your drink. That's right—Big Red.*

THE F WORD: ABOUT FROZEN DRINKS

Frozen drinks are a polarizing topic among those committed to quality drinks. The Daiquiri shacks of America's beach destinations and party towns have done a great disservice to the frozen cocktail. Quite often drinks being served from frozen drink machines are made with commercial mixes and made-up flavors. At their worst, even the booze isn't what you think it is. There are a few notorious drive-through drink stands that serve "Daiquiris" made without rum, and "Margaritas" made with tequila-flavored wine. As you can imagine, this is anathema to the craft cocktail bartender and discriminating consumer alike.

But just because a drink has the consistency of a Slurpee does not mean it must be made from artificial ingredients. A properly made frozen drink can adhere to all the commandments of craft mixology—flavor, balance, freshness, and quality. When you consider the egregious heat and duration of a Texas summer, it becomes all the more imperative to engineer frozen drinks that satisfy as well as they cool.

According to Tomas Estes, the legendary restaurateur and tequila ambassador, "Even though I personally prefer mine on the rocks, a frozen Margarita is a quick way to get a drink into somebody's hands. So it appeals to restaurant operators, including me in some of my restaurants in London and Paris. But it's like anything else, if you put in garbage, you get garbage out. If you put in quality, you get quality out." A frozen Margarita, just like its shaken counterpart, must be made with 100% agave tequila, freshly squeezed lime juice, and good-quality orange liqueur.

The biggest misstep home bartenders make when preparing frozen drinks (besides using inferior-quality mixes) is to take a perfectly delicious drink on the rocks and throw it in the blender. The result is a watery mess, because of all the added dilution from the blended ice. It is important to compensate with additional sweet, sour, and boozy ingredients. Another common problem involves the ice used. If you are using a typical home blender, as opposed to a professional blender such as a Vita-Mix, chances are your blender does not have the capacity to completely crush the large cubes that come from your freezer's ice cube trays. It is best to buy a bag of ice from the convenience store or slightly crush ice from your freezer, as this will give your blender a leg up and result in a smoother texture. The last thing you want in a frozen drink is giant chunks that clog up your sippy straw.

FUN FOR THE WHOLE FAMILY

Makes about eight 8-ounce cocktails

1 cup (8 ounces) 100% agave tequila

1 cup (8 ounces) Cointreau or Paula's Texas Orange

10 ounces freshly squeezed lime juice

4 ounces Simple Syrup *(recipe follows)*

Coarse salt *(optional)*

Lime wedges, for garnish

Combine the tequila, Cointreau, lime juice, and simple syrup in a blender cup and fill with ice until the ice is just covered by the liquid. Blend thoroughly (it may be necessary to add a little bit more ice to achieve the desired slushiness). Pour into goblets, rimmed with coarse salt if you like, and garnish each glass with a lime wedge.

Note: *This recipe is scaled for a Vitamix-style blender with a larger blender pitcher. If your blender has a small pitcher, either blend this recipe in batches or cut it in half.*

SIMPLE SYRUP

Makes about 1½ cups

1 cup filtered water

1 cup sugar

In a small saucepan, bring the water and sugar to a simmer and stir until dissolved. Allow to cool. Bottle and store in the refrigerator for up to 1 month.

TIPSY ENTERTAINING:
TEX-MEX HAPPY HOUR

One of my favorite impromptu parties to throw is a Tex-Mex Happy Hour. A trip to the grocery store, a stop-off at the liquor store, and about an hour in the kitchen and you can throw an easy happy hour that will make quite an impression.

DRINKS:

Margaritas—Frozen, Persimmon, or traditional

Mexican beers

Micheladas

Tequila Slammers

SNACKS:

Tostadas with Guacamole, Salsa, and Chile con Queso

Tipsy's TXTM *(Tex by Tex-Mex)* Brisket Nachos *(page 86)*

TEQUILA SLAMMER

Most Texans are familiar with the ritual of shooting tequila with salt and lime, though we reject this tradition. First, it is a jarring sensory experience. Salt and lime hardly complement good tequila, and were probably adopted originally as a method of making bad tequila more palatable. Although we generally believe that quality tequila should be sipped and not shot, there is a certain celebratory fun to the occasional tequila shooter. We prefer this alternative to salt and lime.

Pinch of ground cinnamon

1½ ounces 100% agave reposado tequila

Orange wedge, for garnish

In the traditional "lick it, slam it, suck it" method, first lick the cinnamon, then shoot the tequila, and lastly suck on the orange wedge.

TIPSY'S TXTM (TEX BY TEX-MEX)
BRISKET NACHOS

Although the nacho may be a staple of Tex-Mex cuisine, there is one way to make it even more Texy: Add brisket. If you want the full effect, it's best to make the refried black beans and the tortilla chips from scratch. Unless you happen to be a pit master, I recommend buying the brisket and barbecue sauce from a reputable source. Because the brisket is going to most likely be reheated for this dish—and because fat tastes so damn good—I recommend buying "moist" brisket for this purpose, moist being a Texas euphemism for meat cut from the fatty end of the brisket. I prefer the brisket from my friends at Austin's Franklin Barbecue, but you probably have your own barbecue joint in mind. If there's one thing to never pick a fight with a Texan about, it's brisket. (It is, however, completely acceptable for a Texan to pick a fight about brisket with a Kansan, Tennessean, or North Carolinian, since they seem to have it all wrong.)

Refried Beans *(page 87)*
Chips *(page 87)*
1 pound fatty brisket, sliced
6 ounces barbecue sauce, or to taste
4 cups shredded white Cheddar cheese
Sour cream, to serve
Guacamole, to serve
Salsa, to serve

Preheat the oven to 350°F. Using a spoon or spatula, spread the refried beans over the fried tortillas. Lay a small piece of brisket on the chips, along with a small squeeze of barbecue sauce. Spread the shredded cheese generously over the chips and bake until the cheese is melted, 8 to 10 minutes. Serve with sour cream, guacamole, and salsa. Save the leftover refried black beans for a delicious bean dip, or for bean and cheese tacos or other uses.

REFRIED BEANS

½ pound bacon, diced

¾ cup diced white onion

8 cloves garlic, minced

4 jalapeño peppers, seeds and ribs removed, diced

2 small or 1 large tomato, diced

2 (15-ounce) cans Goya Frijoles Negros or other black beans

Salt and pepper

Fresh cilantro, chopped *(optional)*

In a hot skillet, preferably cast iron, place the diced bacon and cook until it loses translucency and starts to crisp, 10 to 12 minutes. Add the onion, garlic, and jalapeños. Sauté over medium heat for 3 to 5 minutes, until they start to soften, stirring occasionally to avoid burning the garlic. Add the tomato and cook for a few minutes, until it starts to fall apart. Add the beans and sauté until the mixture thickens, 7 to 10 minutes. Add the salt and pepper and cilantro to taste. Using an immersion blender, puree the beans until mostly smooth with a few identifiable whole and partial beans remaining. Adjust the seasoning as needed. Continue to cook over medium heat for 5 minutes. Allow to cool slightly before serving.

CHIPS

Vegetable oil

12 yellow corn tortillas, cut in half

Coarse salt

Cover the bottom of a deep skillet with about ½ inch of vegetable oil and bring to about 350°F. Test the oil by dropping a piece of tortilla into it—if the tortilla sizzles and floats, the oil is ready. If it sinks, the oil is not hot enough. Fry the tortillas in the hot oil until crispy, about 30 seconds on each side. Set on paper towels to drain and sprinkle with coarse salt while still hot.

MOJITO

Anyone who has dined in public in the half-decade or so immediately before and after the turn of the recent millennium no doubt has run into the Mojito. This early-twentieth-century classic started rearing its head again in nightclubs in such coastal cities as Miami, and soon spread to the landlocked states. Before long, there were entire Cuban-themed bars devoted to the drink, and eventually every chain restaurant in every suburb served some version of the Mojito. As the bartenders grumbled at the new task of stocking and muddling mint, the phenomenon of the Mojito mix emerged, and in many establishments the drink went the way of so many of its cocktail brethren before it—that is, downhill and fast.

The tragedy of the Mojito's popular demise is unfortunate because, when properly made, the drink is delicious, and you'd be hard-pressed to find something more suited to our seemingly endless summer. Fresh lime, ample mint, and good rum are key; Sour mix and Sprite, not so much.

3 large sprigs fresh mint
¾ ounce Simple Syrup *(page 83)*
2 ounces white rum
¾ ounce freshly squeezed lime juice
1 to 1½ ounces carbonated water
Lime wedge, for garnish

Gently muddle two of the mint sprigs and the simple syrup in the bottom of a mixing glass. Add the rum and lime juice. Adjust the amount of syrup to taste. Shake the ingredients vigorously with ice to chill. Strain into an ice-filled Collins glass—crushed ice is best. Top with the carbonated water. Garnish with the remaining mint sprig and the lime wedge and serve with a straw. Some drinkers prefer to leave the muddled mint in the glass; I prefer to strain it out. Utilizing a toothpick after a steak is a worthy endeavor, not so with a cocktail.

WATERMELON MOJITO

Like most classic Sour-formula cocktails, the Mojito is an easy target for market-fresh improvisation. Any number or combination of fresh fruits can be muddled with the mint and other herbs to create an easy seasonal twist. My favorite such variation is made with watermelon, which to me is synonymous with summer and always in the refrigerator during its long season.

4 large sprigs fresh mint

About ½ cup cubed and seeded watermelon

½ to ¾ ounce Simple Syrup *(page 83)*

1½ ounces white rum

¾ ounce freshly squeezed lime juice

1 to 1½ ounces carbonated water

Lime wedge, for garnish

Gently muddle three of the mint sprigs and the watermelon with the simple syrup in the bottom of a mixing glass. Add the rum and lime juice and shake vigorously with ice to chill. You may need to adjust the amount of syrup depending on how sweet your watermelon is. Strain into an ice-filled Collins glass. Top with the carbonated water. Garnish with the remaining mint sprig and the lime wedge and serve with a straw.

CARBONATED WATER

While a bottle of carbonated water from the grocery store will get the job done, I prefer charged water from a soda siphon. Bottled bubble water—especially in plastic bottles—tends to go flat quickly, whereas a siphon of charged water will stay perky in the fridge for a long time. More important, the water coming out of a siphon does so with force and invigorates the drink from the bottom up, as opposed to just sitting on the top of the glass. The standard iSi soda siphon is reasonably inexpensive, and is definitely cost-effective in the long run. Simply fill the siphon with filtered water, charge with a CO_2 cartridge, and refrigerate.

PEAR NOEL

Most so-called holiday cocktails tend to draw on a limited selection of flavors—peppermint, gingerbread, or cream. A few years ago I was asked to create a holiday cocktail for Tito's Handmade Vodka and decided to do something different. Bright and crisp instead of heavy and creamy, this cocktail captures the flavor of the season with crisp pear and citrus and a bit of savory spice. The name is a play on Père Noël, the French name for Santa.

1½ ounces Tito's Handmade Vodka

1½ ounces Mathilde pear liqueur, or similar

½ ounce freshly squeezed lemon juice

1 bar spoon St. Elizabeth Allspice Dram

Slice of fresh pear or lemon twist, for garnish

Combine the vodka, pear liqueur, lemon juice, and allspice dram in a mixing glass and shake vigorously with ice to chill. Strain into a chilled cocktail glass. Garnish with the pear slice or lemon twist.

PIMM'S CUP

PIMM'S CUP

Although the Pimm's Cup is the official cocktail of Wimbledon (if not, in fact, of Britain and her former colonies), its domestic home is the Napoleon House in New Orleans. Pimm's is a low-proof, herbal, gin-based English liqueur with notes of citrus. The Pimm's Cup is a simple combination of Pimm's topped with ginger ale, club soda, or what the Brits call "lemonade," better known as Sprite on this side of the pond. The remarkable feature of this cocktail is the garnish: a cucumber spear, lemon wheel, mint or borage sprig, and any of a host of other fruits and herbs of the season.

The Pimm's Cup is a great platform for improvisation with regional and seasonal flavors. At Houston's Anvil Bar & Refuge, the bartenders muddle the cucumber and spike it with some additional gin. Try muddling some local melon, or give it a dash of your favorite bitters. The Pimm's Cup's low alcohol and bright flavors make it the perfect refreshment for a hot muggy day, be it in New Orleans or Houston.

1½ ounces Pimm's No. 1

3 ounces natural bitter lemon or lemon-lime soda, or ginger ale

Cucumber spear, mint sprig, and fresh seasonal fruit, for garnish

Build the Pimm's and lemon soda over ice in a highball glass. Garnish abundantly with cucumber, herbs, and fruit.

TITO BEVERIDGE

TITO'S HANDMADE VODKA

In an industry where brands are created in boardrooms, slogans are tested on focus groups, and "family recipes" are just as likely to be a fiction, the founding father of Texas distilling is refreshingly, authentically his own self. Unscripted and raw, Tito Beveridge answers to no corporate masters, and you never have to wonder how he feels about a given subject. "There are people who are willing to get out there and stick their nuts on the line and sink their whole life into something," he says about the entrepreneurial spirit. "Then there are other people who are always critical, bringing people down. The critics and haters, these are the people who don't have any nuts to stick on the line and do it themselves."

A native of San Antonio, Beveridge graduated from the University of Texas with a degree in geology and geophysics. "I was in the oil and gas business. Can you imagine going from hanging out with those old coots to hanging out with all the fun and pretty people in the hospitality business?" he jokes of those days.

Beveridge's job necessarily involves a lot of hanging out—and today he is called to do so all over the country—but it has not always been such smooth sailing. When he decided in the 1990s to build a new distillery in Texas, the state liquor authority had no mechanism in place by which to do so. Although it is by no means easy to start up a distillery even now, in those days there was not even a permit to apply for. He encountered obstacles on every level from local to state to federal—even family and friends tried to intervene and get him back on a more conventional path.

In spite of the seemingly insurmountable odds against him—or perhaps because of them—Beveridge was tenacious, parsing code and working with regulators in real time to create the process by which he could set up his operation. In the ensuing decade and a half, Tito's has grown from a cobbled-together still in a shack on scrubland southeast of Austin to a modern production facility that produces vodka that sells in all fifty states.

What does Beveridge make of the state of the craft-distilling movement that he helped to launch? "When I was first getting started, it was impossible to raise money for this," he says. He famously claims to have built the first distillery on maxed-out credit cards. Judging from the flow of capital into liquor start-ups, the times have certainly changed. "On the one hand, I look at this and think, 'This is awesome, so many new products and great people getting

Principles for Success

- **Have an above-average pain tolerance for the long haul.**
- **Grow loyalty in your own hometown first.**
- **Maintain sole ownership of your business if you can.**

into the industry.' It's exciting that there are a lot of little distilleries putting good products out there, though it also makes it more and more competitive. It helps that people are buying American, and buying local." On the other hand, Beveridge compares the growth in craft distilling to the beer industry, in which the vast majority of sales are controlled by multinational companies, with just a tiny share to split between all the independents.

Beveridge explains that many people launching liquor brands dramatically underestimate the vagaries of the marketplace. Getting distribution does not mean the work is through. "Just because we're in fifty states doesn't mean anything; we've got a ton of work to do to get it in all the stores, in all the bars. It costs a fortune to sell your product and tell your story. But you just do it one person at a time. Do it long enough, enough places, it starts working." ✦

RIO STAR SLING

Austin bartender Ben Craven created this contemporary sling to show off the red grapefruits from the Rio Grande Valley. Texas grapefruits are in season from October to late spring and are incredibly sweet and juicy. If using California or other grapefruits, you may need to adjust the sweetness.

**1 ounce gin,
preferably navy strength**

**½ ounce Carpano Antica Formula or
other full-flavored sweet vermouth**

½ ounce Rio Star grapefruit juice

½ ounce freshly squeezed lemon juice

½ ounce Simple Syrup *(page 83)*

2 dashes of Angostura bitters

Dash of grapefruit bitters

1 to 2 ounces carbonated water

Grapefruit wedge, for garnish

Combine the gin, Carpano Antica, grapefruit juice, lemon juice, simple syrup, and both bitters in a mixing glass and shake vigorously with ice to chill. Strain onto fresh ice in a Collins glass and top with the carbonated water. Garnish with the grapefruit wedge.

ROOT BEER "FLOAT"

When absinthe first became legal again in the United States, there was a flood of revivalist efforts to bring back the old-fashioned rituals of absinthe fountains, spoons, sugar cubes, and all the other trappings of absinthe mysticism. Although all of that is good, at the end of the day absinthe is a delicious spirit that can be used in myriad ways, and so with this drink I decided to have some fun with it.

3 ounces Maine Root organic root beer

1 ounce Tenneyson Absinthe Royale or other blanche absinthe

Fill an Collins glass with ice and pour in the root beer. "Float" the absinthe on top of the root beer; it will louche slightly. Stir before drinking.

ROYALE WITH EASE

I created this cocktail for the opening of
Drink.Well.American Pub in Austin.
It's a great "gateway" cocktail for those
who are on the fence about absinthe or
are just trying it for the first time.

1½ ounces **Tenneyson Absinthe Royale**
other blanche absinthe

1½ ounces **freshly squeezed**
grapefruit juice

½ ounce **freshly squeezed lime juice**

1 ounce **Hibiscus "Grenadine"**
(recipe follows)

¼ ounce **St. Elizabeth Allspice Dram**

3 dashes of **Angostura bitters**

Fresh mint sprig, for garnish

Strip of grapefruit zest, for garnish

Combine all the ingredients, except the
mint and zest, in a mixing glass and shake
vigorously with ice to chill. Strain into a
double Old Fashioned glass over crushed
ice and garnish with the mint sprig,
grapefruit zest, and straws.

GRENADINE

The cocktail and soda flavoring known as grenadine takes its name from its primary ingredient, the pomegranate, which translates to "many-seeded apple." This smallish tree produces apple-size fruits filled with hundreds of kernel-like seeds that pop with a burst of tart-sweet juice. As with many classic cocktail ingredients, grenadine suffered a few indignities over the latter half of the twentieth century, and its modern incarnation bears little resemblance to its historic self. Most commercial grenadines are made with high-fructose corn syrup and artificial color and flavor. Traditional grenadine was made from pomegranate juice and cane sugar. Fortunately, with the wide availability of unsweetened pomegranate juice (such as POM Wonderful), it is easy enough to make your own grenadine. Combine equal parts sugar and unsweetened pomegranate juice in a saucepan and bring to a simmer. Stir until the sugar is dissolved and the syrup thickens slightly. Cover and store refrigerated for up to 1 month.

For the hibiscus "grenadine," you will need whole hibiscus flowers, available in the bulk department or Mexican spice section of the grocery store.

HIBISCUS "GRENADINE"

Makes about 2 cups

1 cup sugar
1 cup filtered water
½ ounce (by weight) dried hibiscus flowers
1 ounce vodka *(optional)*

Combine the sugar and water in a saucepan and bring to a simmer. After 1 minute, add the hibiscus flowers and continue simmering the syrup for 2 minutes. Remove from the heat and allow the hibiscus flowers to steep for an additional 10 minutes. Remove the hibiscus flowers using a fine-mesh strainer and allow the mixture to cool. Add 1 ounce of vodka as a preservative, if using. Store refrigerated for up to 1 month.

RUMBLE SOUR

From a little distillery in the unlikeliest of places
comes one of the most intriguing American craft spirits.
Chip Tate, distiller at Balcones Distilling in Waco (page 102), has combined
Mission figs, turbinado sugar, and wildflower honey to create a distillate that defies
categorization. It's made from sugar, but it's not rum; it's made from fruit, but it's
not brandy. What it is, is delicious, and this is a great way to try it in a classic Sour.
Each bottle of Rumble is hand numbered and made seasonally from entirely
natural ingredients, so slight distinctions emerge with each batch.

2 ounces Balcones Rumble
¾ ounce freshly squeezed lemon juice
½ ounce Orgeat *(page 109)*
1 small egg white *(following page)*

Combine all the ingredients in a mixing
glass and shake without ice for a few moments
to start the emulsion. Add ice and shake
vigorously to ensure the proper, enduring
frothy texture. Strain into a chilled coupe glass.

EGGS

In the early history of American beverages—when a housekeeping book was more common than a cocktail guide—there was an abundance of drinks that combined eggs and alcohol. Some of them, such as caudles and syllabubs, would not likely please the contemporary palate. But as the cocktail came into fashion and displaced some of those more primitive drinks, eggs maintained a prominent role in cocktail manufacture well into the twentieth century. Some of the most famous American drinks involved eggs or egg whites, such as the Ramos Gin Fizz, Whiskey Sour, Sherry Flip, Pisco Sour, and Silver Fizz. Over time, however, eggs fell out of fashion, especially with the industrialization of the American food system in the second half of the twentieth century. The greater the distance that came between Americans and their eggs, the less likely you were to see them appear in cocktails, and the more likely consumers were to fear raw eggs as being unsafe for consumption. To be certain, there can be dangers associated with using raw eggs, but it's not eggs per se that are potentially hazardous. Yard eggs or farmers' market eggs, for example, are substantially less likely to contain salmonella than are commercial eggs. Fresh eggs are safer than old eggs. When properly handled, they are generally safe in cocktails (unless you have a compromised immune system, in which case pasteurized egg whites are an option).

Several factors converge in the egg's favor. First, high-proof alcohol is a natural antimicrobial. Second, many egg cocktails include citrus juice, whose low pH also has germ-killing properties. Lastly, most egg cocktails require just the egg white. Deleterious bacteria, if present at all, tend to reside in the yolk or the egg's shell. If you are concerned about safety, "sanitize" your eggs with a spritz from a spray bottle of vodka or gin! Eggs add body and texture to a cocktail—buy quality fresh eggs and use them properly, and you are in for a classic tipular treat. ❦

CHIP TATE

BALCONES DISTILLING

It may come as a bit of a surprise that some of the most celebrated small-batch American whiskey originates from a tiny distillery under a bridge in an industrial section of Waco, Texas.

Chip Tate, like most craft distillers, came about it by a circuitous path. Tate was born in Lynchburg, Virginia, where he spent his formative years, save for a brief stint when his dad's job took the family to Germany. As a child, Tate was always adventurous in the kitchen and was baking his own bread by the time he got to high school. His early interest in yeast and fermentation would prove fortuitous.

After graduating from high school, Tate studied engineering and philosophy at the College of William and Mary. After college, Chip decided to enroll in the Presbyterian seminary. Although he did not intend to become a minister, he did use his time in seminary to practice that ancient monastic art of brewing beer. Graduating with a masters of divinity, Chip moved to South Bend, Indiana, where he started working in a local brewery.

In 2002, his wife's job moved them to Waco, where he took a job at Baylor University. When the grind of academic politics finally pushed him to the brink, he set out on his own. Although he had long dreamed of opening a brewery, it was in Waco that he had the vision of founding a Texas whiskey tradition. "After planning a brewery for ten years," he explains, "unbeknownst to me, I realized all the pieces were already in place to start a distillery." With business partner Stephen Germer, he started building Balcones Distilling in the summer of 2008.

The distillery was built on a shoestring budget. "We were drastically underfunded," Tate says of the early days. "I think we built an entire distillery for less than some start-ups spend on one piece of equipment. It was an all-in attitude."

Balcones, true to the words on its label, set out to create "original" Texas whiskeys. "It's about something that starts with a local, artistic, Texas terroir concept," Tate says of the creative process behind his distillery's products. "The spirit has to learn everything it can from the tradition, but tweak it to make something that's unique, interesting, and hopefully great."

The first two releases from Balcones were Baby Blue, a blue corn whiskey, and Rumble, a unique spirit made from wildflower honey, turbinado sugar, and Mission figs (see Rumble Sour, page 100). Brimstone, a scrub oak–smoked corn whiskey, followed suit, along with a Texas single malt that has gained a cult following.

"Our whiskeys make sense that they're made in Texas. Our malt whiskey is about the heat. Our corn whiskey is about the corn. Tex-Mex, masa, corn tortillas, are all a big part of Texas cuisine," Tate explains. "Our Brimstone smoked whiskey makes sense when you think about Texas barbecue. That oak is not the oak that I grew up with in Virginia. It tastes different; it's grown in a totally different environment."

Tate stresses the importance of honoring traditional whiskey-making methods while not letting those traditions restrict creativity. "Rules and styles and traditions are tricky," he says. "They're good. But when they start being confining, if you can ask yourself the question: 'Is there any reason not to do something other than because it's never been done before?' and if the answer is no, then get over it."

That sense of curiosity and Tate and Germer's all-in effort paid off, earning Double Gold medals for their spirits, and Craft Whiskey Distiller of the Year designation for their distiller. The accolades have brought Balcones to a national and international audience, but the spirits never lose their distinct sense of place. "All of our whiskeys taste like the things from which they're made, flavors that we think belong to Texas whiskey." The critics and fans alike seem to agree. ❧

SANDIA 🍸

This drink was the 2009 winner of the Official Drink of Austin contest. It was created by Texas bartender Nate Wales for La Condesa restaurant and is one of my favorite cocktails of summer. When local watermelons are at their peak of sweetness, the agave nectar is not necessary, though can be added to taste to adjust for less-sweet melons, or whenever a sweeter cocktail is preferred.

2 ounces Tito's Handmade Vodka

¾ ounce St-Germain elderflower liqueur

1½ ounces watermelon water *(see Note)*

¾ ounce freshly squeezed lime juice

¼ ounce agave nectar *(optional)*

Watermelon wedge, for garnish

Combine all the ingredients, except the watermelon wedge, in a mixing glass and shake vigorously with ice to chill. Strain into a chilled cocktail glass and garnish with the watermelon wedge.

Note: *You can create the watermelon water a number of ways: Crush watermelon with a muddler and push through a strainer; run it through a pulp extractor–style juicer; or blend lightly in a blender and pour through a strainer.*

SANGRIA ROSA

For summer entertainment, there is nothing more easy to make, enjoyable to drink, and beautiful to behold as this simple, elegant rosé sangria. Select fruit that is in season, preferably local, and at the peak of ripeness. The fresh fruit juices that infuse with the wine and spirits are the essence of sangria. In summertime in Texas, we have a long and glorious season for melons and peaches, which make for excellent sangria. The following recipe is designed to fill an average-size-watermelon "punch bowl," and can easily be doubled or quadrupled depending on the size of your gathering.

2 (750 ml) bottles rosé wine
(I like Charles & Charles)

2 cups St-Germain elderflower liqueur

1 quart cut-up seasonal fruit and berries

1 watermelon, hollowed out, to serve *(optional)*

Large block of ice

1 cup carbonated water

Combine the wine and St-Germain with the cut fruit in a 1-gallon container. Place in the refrigerator and allow the fruit to macerate for several hours, if time allows. Transfer to a punch bowl or a hollowed-out watermelon and add the block of ice. Add the carbonated water just before service. Serve with a ladle, making sure each portion is garnished with some of the cut fruit.

SHOWGIRL

I created this drink for the 2011 Cocktail World Cup regional quarter-final. I was one of the winners of the local round and proceeded to New York, where it did not fare as well.* But this drink has always been a "winner" wherever I've served it and is one of my favorite vodka drinks in the tiki style.

1½ ounces vodka

¼ ounce passion fruit syrup or puree *(if using puree, the sweetness may need to be adjusted)*

½ ounce Orgeat (recipe follows)

½ ounce freshly squeezed lime juice

1 bar spoon St. Elizabeth Allspice Dram

2 dashes of Bitter Truth Jerry Thomas's Own Decanter Bitters

Several sprigs fresh seasonal herbs and citrus zest, for garnish

Combine all the ingredients, except the herbs, in a mixing glass and shake vigorously with ice to chill. Strain into a highball glass or tiki mug filled with crushed ice, and garnish with a "headdress" of herbs and citrus zest—mint, basil, lemon verbena, lavender, kaffir lime, edible flowers—whatever you have on hand. Give this beauty what she deserves.

*On a brighter note, my colleague Nate Wales—also from Austin—did advance in this round, and he and Team USA took second place in the Cocktail World Cup in New Zealand.

ORGEAT

Orgeat (pronounced "or-zhat") is an almond-flavored syrup that was a favorite of the famous tiki bartenders. It adds an elegant suppleness to cocktails, and is an essential ingredient in the classic Mai Tai. Although there are now a few varieties of commercially available orgeat, it is easy enough to make at home.

Makes about 2 cups

2 cups raw whole almonds

1 cup warm water, plus 1 cup cold water *(filtered water is recommended)*

2 cups evaporated cane juice or granulated sugar

Dash of rose water

Dash of orange flower water

In a mixing bowl, cover the almonds with the warm water and soak for 30 minutes. Discard the water. Pulverize the almonds in a food processor and return to the bowl. Cover with the cold water and allow to steep for at least 6 hours or overnight. Press through a chinois or strain through several layers of cheesecloth, then discard the almond pulp. In a small saucepan, bring the almond water and sugar to a simmer and stir until the sugar dissolves. Season with the rose water and orange flower water. Chill and store refrigerated for up to 1 month.

SHOWGIRL

SILK ROAD

I know that the caravaners traveling along ancient trade routes probably suffered dearly for cocktails, but this is what they might have drunk given the opportunity. It is at once sweet and tart from the raspberries, spiced with young ginger and cooling herbs.

6 raspberries

4 leaves (1 smallish sprig) **fresh cilantro**

1 sprig fresh mint

1 bar spoon Simple Syrup (page 83)

1½ ounces pisco

¾ ounce Domaine de Canton ginger liqueur

Lemon twist, for garnish

Muddle five of the raspberries and the cilantro, mint, and simple syrup in the bottom of a mixing glass. Add the pisco and ginger liqueur; shake vigorously with ice and fine-strain into a chilled cocktail glass. Garnish with the lemon twist and the remaining whole raspberry.

ST-GERMAIN COCKTAIL

It is not often that cocktail enthusiasts have the opportunity to watch a classic cocktail being born. At the risk of claiming to see the future, I believe that is what is happening with the St-Germain Cocktail. Although it is an aperitif in the European style, it is infinitely refreshing on a hot Texas day. As an aperitif, it is the perfect punctuation mark between a day of work and an evening of dinner and leisure. At week's end, it is the ultimate brunch cocktail. Indeed, I envision a day when the Mimosa quakes in fear of the St-Germain Cocktail, knowing that it has been outclassed by a deliciously nuanced newcomer.

---

2 ounces champagne, Prosecco, or other brut *(dry)* sparkling wine

2 ounces carbonated water

1½ ounces St-Germain elderflower liqueur

Strip of lemon zest, for garnish

Fill a Collins glass with ice. Add the champagne and carbonated water, being careful to pour down the side of the glass to maximize bubble preservation. Add the St-Germain. Using a bar spoon, stir gently to combine the ingredients. Garnish with the lemon zest, expressed over the top of the cocktail.

ST-GERMAIN

St-Germain is a liqueur made in France from wild elderflower blossoms. Although elderflower is commonly used in nonalcoholic syrups in Europe, this product was the first to incorporate the flower into a liqueur. The most delicate essence of elderflower is captured in a grape *eau de vie* and lightly sweetened with cane sugar. The resulting liqueur offers up an elegant bouquet of honeysuckle and ripe fruit notes, such as lychee, pear, and grapefruit. Although the St-Germain Cocktail is the most elemental expression of St-Germain, the liqueur can be used in a virtually unlimited variety of cocktails.

STRAWBERRY-LIME RICKEY

A traditional Rickey is made with gin, lime juice, and club soda—not to be confused with a Gimlet, which is made with preserved lime cordial. Here is a sweet Rickey variation that marries Texas gin with fresh strawberries.

3 large, ripe strawberries

½ lime, cut into quarters

¼ to ½ ounce Simple Syrup *(page 83)*

2 ounces Waterloo Gin

Club soda

Lime wheel, for garnish

Strawberry slice, for garnish

In the bottom of a mixing glass, muddle the strawberries, lime wedges, and simple syrup. Adjust the amount of syrup depending on the sweetness of your strawberries. Add the gin and shake vigorously with ice to chill. Strain into an Old Fashioned glass over fresh ice. Top with a spritz of club soda. Garnish with the lime wheel and strawberry slice.

TEXAS SIPPER

This spring refresher utilizes Tito's Vodka as a platform for the flavor of Texas's red grapefruits, sweetened with a little St-Germain, which also has a prominent grapefruit note. It's easy to make this drink in a pitcher when entertaining friends. This cocktail comes from Austin cocktail enthusiast Lisa Nuccio.

1½ ounces Tito's Handmade Vodka

½ ounce St-Germain elderflower liqueur

1½ ounces freshly squeezed red grapefruit juice

1 ounce carbonated water *(or grapefruit soda, such as Squirt, if you have it)*

Fresh mint sprig, for garnish

Combine the vodka, St-Germain, and grapefruit juice in a mixing glass and shake vigorously with ice to chill. Strain onto fresh ice in a rocks glass and top with the carbonated water. Garnish with the mint sprig.

STRAWBERRY-LIME RICKEY

STONEWALL SOUR

The small Hill Country town of Stonewall sits between Fredericksburg and Johnson City on Highway 290. President Lyndon Baines Johnson's ranch, affectionately known as the "Texas White House," is just down the road. This is country where Texas peaches thrive, and this cocktail captures their essence with a sweet-sour peach *gastrique*.

2 or 3 chunks ripe cantaloupe, plus 1 small wedge for garnish

4 medium-size fresh basil leaves

½ ounce freshly squeezed lime juice

½ ounce Simple Syrup *(page 83)*

1½ ounces pisco

3 dashes of Angostura bitters

1 ounce Peach Gastrique *(recipe follows)*

In a mixing glass, muddle the cantaloupe chunks, 3 of the basil leaves, the lime juice, and simple syrup. Add the pisco, bitters, and peach *gastrique*. Shake vigorously with ice and strain into a chilled cocktail glass. Garnish with the cantaloupe wedge and remaining basil leaf.

PEACH GASTRIQUE

Gastriques are sweet-sour reduction syrups that are great for adding an acidic bite to cocktails. In the times before modern produce distribution, vinegar might have been used to give cocktails a sour note in the absence of fresh citrus. *Makes about ½ cup*

¼ cup white vinegar

½ cup peach nectar

2 tablespoons raw sugar

2 teaspoons local honey

Combine the vinegar and nectar in a small saucepan, and bring to a simmer. Add the sugar and honey, and reduce the mixture by half. Remove from the heat and allow to cool. Store refrigerated for up to 1 month.

THAI SPRING

This cocktail can be made straight from the garden. Kaffir lime leaves make for an intriguing cocktail herb and a beautiful and unexpected garnish. While the choice of vodka is up to you, the unique profile of Treaty Oak rum is essential for this cocktail.

....

**2 wedges ripe tomato,
or 2 plum or pear tomatoes**

2 kaffir lime leaves

¾ ounce Simple Syrup *(page 83)*

¾ ounce freshly squeezed lime juice

1½ ounces Texas vodka

½ ounce Treaty Oak Platinum Rum

....

In the bottom of a mixing glass, muddle the tomato, one of the kaffir lime leaves, and the simple syrup. Add the lime juice, vodka, and rum and shake vigorously with ice to chill and invigorate the ingredients. Strain into a chilled cocktail glass and garnish with the remaining kaffir lime leaf.

The Collins is one of those few drink categories whose fame is such that it comes with its own eponymous glass. A simple combination of a base spirit, a sweetener, and lemon juice topped with club soda, the possibilities for innovation are virtually endless. The Tom Collins—originally made with gin—dates to the end of the nineteenth century, and was named after the "Old Tom" gin that was popular at the time.

COLLINS

TOM COLLINS

1½ ounces gin

¾ ounce freshly squeezed lemon juice

1 ounce Simple Syrup *(page 83)*

1 to 2 ounces carbonated water

Combine the gin, lemon juice, and simple syrup in a mixing glass with ice and shake vigorously to chill. Strain onto fresh ice in a Collins glass. Top with the carbonated water.

HILL COUNTRY COLLINS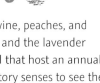

Although the primary exports of the Texas Hill Country are wine, peaches, and barbecue, there are a few other up-and-coming attractions, and the lavender industry is one of them. The town of Blanco is one of several that host an annual Lavender Festival. It is as pleasing to the eyes as to the olfactory senses to see the fields and hillsides of our Hill Country towns cultivated with lavender. Not just for sachets anymore, lavender is an herb that functions well in cocktails and grows enduringly in your yard, regardless of the oppressive heat.

1 small or ½ large ripe peach, cut into chunks

½ ounce Simple Syrup *(page 83)*

2 sprigs fresh lavender

1½ ounces Texas gin

¾ ounce freshly squeezed lemon juice

1 to 2 ounces carbonated water

In the bottom of a mixing glass, muddle the peach, simple syrup, and one of the lavender sprigs. You may need to adjust the amount of syrup depending on the sweetness of your peach. Add the gin and lemon juice. Shake vigorously with ice to chill, and strain onto fresh ice in a Collins glass. Top with the carbonated water and garnish with the remaining lavender sprig.

ELDERFLOWER COLLINS

I adapted this drink from my friend Adam Harris, a fabulous Texas bartender who is best known for his long stint as the flag bearer in Texas for Maker's Mark, and all things Kentucky bourbon.

1½ ounces Maker's Mark Kentucky Straight Bourbon Whisky

¾ ounce St-Germain elderflower liqueur

¾ ounce freshly squeezed lemon juice

1 to 2 ounces carbonated water

Real maraschino cherry, for garnish

Lemon wheel, for garnish

Combine the bourbon, St-Germain, and lemon juice in a mixing glass with ice and shake vigorously to chill. Strain onto fresh ice in a Collins glass and top with the carbonated water. Garnish with the maraschino cherry and lemon wheel "flag."

CALM COLLINS

Enjoy the mildly sedative effect of this bedtime Collins. For a Sean Collins, omit the chamomile syrup and use simple syrup instead.

2 ounces Irish whiskey *(also works well with blended Scotch)*

¾ ounce freshly squeezed lemon juice

½ ounce Chamomile Syrup *(recipe follows)*

1½ to 2 ounces carbonated water

Lemon wheel, for garnish

Combine the whiskey, lemon juice, and chamomile syrup in a mixing glass and shake vigorously with ice to chill. Strain onto fresh ice in a Collins glass; top with the carbonated water. Garnish with the lemon wheel.

CHAMOMILE SYRUP

Makes about 1½ cups

....

1 cup filtered water

1 cup sugar

½ ounce *(by weight)* **dried chamomile blossoms**

....

In a small saucepan, bring the water and sugar to a simmer. Once the sugar has dissolved, stir in the chamomile blossoms and allow to simmer gently until a pronounced chamomile flavor emerges, about 8 minutes. Strain the syrup through a fine-mesh strainer or cheesecloth, pressing the blossoms gently to release more liquid. Allow to cool; store refrigerated for up to 1 month.

TEXAS GIN

Although modern gin as we know it dates back only to the late nineteenth century, gin's ancestors were in large-scale production by the 1600s, and juniper has been infused into spirits since the middle ages. Gin is a botanical spirit and shares the ancient apothecary tradition of gathering local herbs, roots, spices, and other ingredients and distilling them for their purported medicinal benefits. The most common style of gin today is London dry, which utilizes juniper as its predominant botanical. Other botanicals include lemon zest, orris root, coriander, angelica, cassia, fennel, and cardamom among others. Since this style took hold in the United States, there was little interest among American distillers to create gins with a regional profile. However, that is starting to change in Texas.

Waterloo gin, for example, is produced in Austin at Treaty Oak Distilling. A base spirit of wheat and corn is distilled through a botanical-packed column. Although it technically meets the requirements to be called London dry gin, this spirit is made for the Texas palate—local grapefruit, lavender, and pecan enhance the conventional botanical blend of juniper and coriander.

Roxor Artisan Gin is the brainchild of noted Texas chef Robert del Grande and Don Short, a former Coca-Cola executive. Del Grande formulated the botanical mix to include Texas grapefruit and lime, as well as hibiscus. The profile is very citrus-forward, with juniper receding into the background. Both were launched in 2011.

DANIEL BARNES

TREATY OAK DISTILLING

"My primary passions in life are whiskey, music, sneakers, and chicken-fried steak," Daniel Barnes told me. "And my wife and children, of course," he clarified.

Barnes hails from the west Texas town of Menard, near San Angelo, where his parents ran a motel and café called the Navajo Inn. While most of his high school classmates were grabbing a few extra minutes of shut-eye, Barnes spent his mornings preparing the chicken-fried steaks for the lunch crowd at the family's restaurant. After school, he was back prepping "CFS" for the dinner clientele.

"My graduating class at Menard High consisted of forty-two seniors," Barnes reminisced. "Needless to say, Austin was a change of pace." When the Barnes clan moved to the Dripping Springs area, Barnes started at the University of Texas and eventually found himself working at the Four Seasons, where he continued his food and beverage education in a more formal environment than the Navajo Inn.

He met Rachel, the future Mrs. Barnes, on Sixth Street outside the old Bates Motel. They married in 2003. In 2006, he started Graham-Barnes Distilling (now Treaty Oak Distilling) with Bruce Graham, Rachel's stepdad and the man who built the company's first still. "We had a hunch that distilling would take off in Texas," Barnes said of their early days. At the time, you could count Texas distillers on one hand. The first bottles of Treaty Oak Rum started hitting shelves in 2007.

"A lot of people look at getting into this industry because they just think it is big profits and partying all the time," Barnes said. "But it's a lot of hard work, a lot of behind-the-scenes business beyond just distilling rum. Everything about this business is much harder than anyone thinks it's going to be going in. Of course, we do our fair share of partying.

"It's exciting to see the average Joe Public get involved in and gain understanding of the craft side of spirits, instead of getting caught up in the marketing schemes of national companies," Barnes said of the state of the market. "The more attention craft spirits get, the more creative we can get as producers." And created they have. After the initial launch, Treaty Oak Distilling went on to release Waterloo

No. 9, one of the first two Texas gins. Graham's Texas Tea followed, along with Starlite Vodka, aged versions of the company's rum and gin and numerous other projects.

When I asked Barnes to describe the perfect meal, he laid out his vision of chicken-fried steak, washed down with this Tejas Libre. ✦

TEJAS LIBRE

....

2 ounces Treaty Oak Platinum Rum

2 lime wedges

1 to 2 ounces Dublin Dr Pepper

....

To an ice-filled Collins glass, add the rum and a squeeze of one lime wedge. Top with the Dublin Dr Pepper and garnish with the other lime wedge.

TREATY OAK COCKTAIL

The historic, once majestic, Treaty Oak stands in a small square just west of downtown Austin. It is estimated to be nearly five centuries old, and it is significant to the folklore of both modern Texas and the natives who came before. In the late 1980s the tree suffered from a brutal act of vandalism, and the rescue effort to save the tree became a national news story. Pruned pieces of the tree were sold off as all manner of trinkets, and people from all over sent get-well cards to the infirm oak. The Treaty Oak survived, mangled but resilient. Businesses from banks to booze have been inspired by the symbol, and this cocktail was made to be the "official" drink of Treaty Oak Rum.

2 ounces **Treaty Oak Rum**
¾ ounce **Rosemary Syrup** *(see below)*
¾ ounce **freshly squeezed lime juice**
½ ounce **Paula's Texas Orange**
Yellow Chartreuse liqueur
Fresh rosemary sprig, for garnish

Combine the rum, syrup, lime juice, and Paula's Texas Orange in a mixing glass with ice and shake vigorously to chill. Strain into a chilled cocktail glass that has been rinsed with the Yellow Chartreuse. Garnish with the rosemary sprig.

HERB SYRUPS

For most herb syrups, start with Simple Syrup (page 83) or Raw Sugar Syrup (page 135) while still hot, or bring it to a low simmer in a saucepan. Woody herbs such as rosemary and oregano can withstand more heat than can soft herbs such as basil and mint. Steep the herbs in the hot syrup until the desired flavor emerges—prominently herb-y but still fresh and alive, between 5 and 10 minutes. Strain out the herbs and allow the syrup to cool. Store refrigerated for up to 1 month.

WATERMELON WHISKEY SOUR

Part julep, part sour, this cocktail is a recipe for summer refreshment. It can easily be made in a large batch to entertain a group. Keep in mind that watermelons are temperamental, and vary widely in sweetness based on variety and time of year. Be sure to taste the watermelon before using, and again in the cocktail, and adjust with Simple Syrup (page 83) as needed.

**1 cup watermelon chunks, or
2 ounces pressed watermelon juice**

2 sprigs fresh mint

2 sprigs fresh basil

**¾ ounce St-Germain
elderflower liqueur**

1½ ounces bourbon

½ ounce freshly squeezed lemon juice

In a mixing glass, muddle the watermelon with one of the mint sprigs, one of the basil sprigs, and the St-Germain. Add the bourbon and lemon juice. Shake vigorously with ice to chill. Strain onto crushed ice in a double Old Fashioned glass. Garnish with the remaining sprigs of mint and basil.

WABBIT SMASH

One of my favorite cocktail spots in Texas lies not in a cool restored warehouse in a hip nightlife district, but in a former big-box restaurant site in the parking lot of a strip mall in Plano. Local bartender Sean Conner helped open Whiskey Cake, and this cocktail came to him while watching the Sunday morning cartoons with his kids. "One of my favorite cartoons is Bugs Bunny," he explained.

1 (1-inch) piece ginger, peeled and chopped into ⅛-inch dice

¾ ounce Honey Syrup (page 64)

2 ounces Bombay Sapphire gin

¾ ounce freshly squeezed lemon juice

1 ounce fresh carrot juice

Fresh mint sprig, for garnish

In the bottom of a mixing glass, muddle the ginger and honey syrup. Add the gin, lemon juice, and carrot juice and shake vigorously with ice to chill. Strain onto fresh ice in a double Old Fashioned glass. Garnish with the mint sprig.

BIG AND BOOZY

Whether classic or contemporary, thes
spirit-forward cocktails showcase bold
flavors and stout ingredients for mome
that call for a potent tipple

Technique Tip: Glass Rimming

The most common rimmed glass a Texan is likely
to encounter is the one holding a Margarita. The glass
is typically dipped into a moistened sponge followed by a
dunk into a plate of kosher salt. The problem with this method
is twofold—first, the aerial approach of the glass results in as
much salt on the inside rim as on the outside. Once the cocktail
is poured into the glass, the rimming ingredient on the inside of
the glass is now in the cocktail, affecting flavor. Second, the aerial
approach results in a 360-degree coating of the glass rim, which
means that there is no way to avoid the rimming ingredient.
The better way to do it is to moisten only the outside rim of the
glass with a piece of cut fruit appropriate to the cocktail—for
a Margarita, a lime. Then gently "roll" the moistened rim in a
shallow plate of the rimming ingredient, such that it adheres
only to the outside of the glass. You can go for the full circle,
or only rim part of the glass, to your liking.

ABBEVILLE DAIQUIRI

The C. S. Steen sugar works has operated in the tiny southern Louisiana town of Abbeville since 1910. I discovered this product during my annual pilgrimage to Tales of the Cocktail, the international cocktail and culinary festival held in New Orleans each summer. Although more commonly found on the breakfast table than the bar, Steen's makes for an intriguing cocktail sweetener. I love the deep connection that Texans have with our neighbors to the east. The rich culture and people of Louisiana flow sweetly throughout Texas, like so much Steen's over a biscuit. This cocktail is inspired by the Hemingway Daiquiri.

1½ ounces Treaty Oak rum or other white rum

¼ ounce Luxardo maraschino liqueur

¾ ounce freshly squeezed lime juice

½ ounce Steen's 100% Pure Cane Syrup

½ ounce freshly squeezed grapefruit juice

Dash of Peychaud's Bitters, for floater

Cinnamon-Sugar-Cayenne rim *(recipe follows)*

Combine the rum, maraschino liqueur, lime juice, syrup, and grapefruit juice in a mixing glass and shake vigorously with ice to chill. Strain into a chilled cocktail glass rimmed with a cinnamon-sugar-cayenne rim (see Technique Tip: Glass Rimming, page 130). Finish with the dash of Peychaud's Bitters floated on top of the cocktail.

CINNAMON-SUGAR-CAYENNE RIM

2 tablespoons sugar or evaporated cane juice

½ teaspoon ground cinnamon

¼ teaspoon cayenne pepper

Combine all the ingredients in a small bowl and stir well. Store in a covered container in the spice cabinet.

ABSINTHE YVETTE

Crème Yvette is a historic liqueur that was made by the Charles Jacquin distillery in Philadelphia starting in the 1890s. By the 1960s the product had fallen out of popular favor and was eventually discontinued. Due to the lobbying efforts of cocktail and spirit preservationists such as Ted Haigh, the product was finally brought back to life by the Cooper Spirits Company's Rob Cooper, whose family owned the Jacquin distillery and the formula for Crème Yvette. Crème Yvette is now made in France from blackberries, currants, raspberries, wild strawberries, and violets.

Traditionally, absinthe drinkers would have sweetened absinthe with a sugar ube. Today's absinthes are of high enough quality that they only require sugar if the drinker prefers it, which I do not. Here is a little frappé-style cocktail that marries absinthe to Crème Yvette.

1 ounce traditional verte absinthe
¾ ounce Crème Yvette

Fill a footed highball glass with crushed ice; strain off any water that settles to the bottom. Pour the absinthe over the ice—it will begin to louche. Pour the Crème Yvette over the top. Due to its relative weight it will trickle down and settle in the bottom of the glass, lacing the absinthe with its flavor as it stratifies.

ACCIDENTAL TOURIST

In the late 2000-aughts, a mystifying cocktail called the Trinidad Sour emerged from Brooklyn bartender Giuseppe Gonzales. Angostura bitters took the lead this time as the base ingredient, inverting its typical ration of dashes and drops. Texans who know that we don't sell liquor at the grocery store may be surprised that Angostura bitters clock in at 44.7% alcohol by volume, comparable to a bottle of bourbon—but we can buy it at our neighborhood H-E-B grocery store. It may not be conventional, but the Trinidad Sour proved that "Ango" can serve in the foundational role. From its origins in New York, the drink gave birth to an entire mini-genre of "Kill 'Em All" cocktails, in which obscure or pungent ingredients were recruited in proportions hitherto thought unnatural. I first learned of the Trinidad from a friend of mine as he attempted (under the influence, it can be assumed) to text me instructions, and getting it entirely wrong. Some mistakes, of course, taste great, and so you get the Accidental Tourist.

---

1 ounce Rhum Barbancourt 5-Star

1 ounce Peychaud's Bitters

½ ounce Fernet Branca

½ ounce Lime Cordial *(page 62)*

½ ounce Raw Sugar Syrup *(recipe follows)*

½ ounce freshly squeezed grapefruit juice

Dash of Angostura bitters

Combine all the ingredients in a mixing glass and shake exuberantly with ice in an effort to coax a loving, lasting relationship out of the ingredients. Strain into a chilled rocks glass.

RAW SUGAR SYRUP

Makes about 2½ cups

1 cup filtered water
2 cups raw sugar or evaporated cane juice

In a small saucepan, bring the water and sugar to a simmer and stir until dissolved. Allow to cool. Bottle and store refrigerated for up to 1 month.

BITTERS

Cocktail bitters are to drink-making what salt, pepper, and the spice cabinet are to cooking—you don't necessarily notice that they're there, but in their absence you would notice that something was missing. Bitters are generally used in drops and dashes to season cocktails, though can sometimes take the lead, such as in the Trinidad Sour or the Accidental Tourist (page 134).

The manufacture of bitters is, of course, a proprietary process, so it is impossible to know what exactly goes into making any particular label. Generally speaking, bitters are made by macerating herbs, spices, fruits, or other botanicals into a high-proof neutral spirit. Historically bitters were used for their purported medicinal benefit, and at one time every local apothecary carried his own formula for bitters in addition to a few national brands.

Over time bitters began to be used for properties less therapeutic than gastronomical, and a few regional and national brands emerged to service the cocktail market. But the party would be crashed by Prohibition—very few labels would survive the Noble Experiment.

Although bitters attained a decidedly recreational status, there are some vestiges of their medicinal past. To this day they are classified as "nonpotable," despite their high alcohol content—any Texan can attest to not being able to buy a bottle of whiskey at the grocery store, but being able to buy a bottle of bitters, despite Angostura's being higher in alcohol than Jim Beam. For many decades Angostura was the only brand of bitters that was widely available in the United States. Fortunately for cocktail enthusiasts there is once again a profusion of bitters on the market.

Essential Bitters

Angostura Aromatic Bitters
(Trinidad)

Peychaud's Bitters
(Frankfort, Kentucky)

Orange bitters—Angostura or Gary Regan's No. 6
(Frankfort, Kentucky)

My Favorite Bitters

Bittermens Tiki Bitters
(Brooklyn, New York)

Bitter Truth Jerry Thomas's Own Decanter Bitters
(Germany)

Bad Dog Barcraft Sarsaparilla Dry Bitters *(Austin, Texas)*

BROWN SUGAR SNOW

Pam Prichard is one of my favorite Texas bar owners. After twenty-five years of working in the laboratory environment in her native Southern California, she moved to Austin to pursue a new career in tavern keeping. Despite never actually having worked in a bar, Pam opened the Tigress, the best usage of 690 square feet in Texas. Despite the bar's diminutive size, Pam's hospitality is as big as Texas—there are very few of Texas's top bartenders who haven't pulled a "guest" shift behind her bar. This is Pam's signature drink, which she created for the opening of the Blind Pig in Louisville, Kentucky.

1½ ounces 100-proof rye whiskey
1 ounce Averna Amaro
½ ounce freshly squeezed lemon juice
¼ ounce Brown Sugar Syrup
(recipe follows)

Combine all the ingredients in a mixing glass with ice and shake vigorously to chill. Strain into a chilled cocktail glass.

BITTER BREAKUP

Bitter and sweet, this is a Valentine's Day drink for the recently single.

1½ ounces Tito's Handmade Vodka
½ ounce Campari
¼ ounce Cointreau or Paula's Texas Orange
2 dashes of Peychaud's Bitters
½ bar spoon Luxardo maraschino liqueur
Flamed orange "coin," for garnish

Combine the vodka, Campari, Cointreau, bitters, and maraschino liqueur in a mixing glass with ice and stir to chill. Strain into a chilled cocktail glass and garnish with the flamed orange "coin."

BROWN SUGAR SYRUP

Makes about 1½ cups

1 cup filtered water
1 cup dark brown sugar

In a small saucepan, bring the water and sugar to a simmer and stir until the sugar is dissolved. Allow to cool. Bottle and store refrigerated for up to 1 month.

CZECH MIX

Central Texas is studded with towns whose names, such as West, belie the unusual-sounding surnames of their denizens. This is the Czech Belt, where thousands of Eastern European immigrants settled after passing through Galveston, the Ellis Island of the Gulf of Mexico. In some communities, Czech is taught as a second language in public schools. Becherovka is a Czech liqueur with a predominant clove note; Big Red is a Texas soda in production since 1937. For this recipe, they're inseparable.

2 ounces Becherovka

3 ounces Big Red

Strip of clove-studded orange zest, for garnish

Add the Becherovka to an ice-filled highball glass. Top with the Big Red. Garnish with the clove-studded orange peel by first holding the orange zest by its sides, lighting the center part of the clove, and expressing the oils out of the orange peel through the flame and onto the top of the drink.

FOOL'S GOLD

Joe Eifler created this cocktail to make use of some fabulous fresh, local, unpasteurized apple cider we'd gotten at the fall farmers' market. The spicy rye whiskey tones down the sweetness of the cider. Cynar is an Italian bitter, or *amaro*, made with artichokes.

1½ ounces Wild Turkey Rye

2 ounces apple cider

¾ ounce Cynar

½ ounce freshly squeezed lemon juice

1 bar spoon Simple Syrup *(page 83)*

2 dashes of London dry gin

Apple slice, for garnish

Combine the rye, cider, Cynar, lemon juice, and simple syrup in a mixing glass and shake vigorously with ice to chill. You may need to adjust the amount of syrup depending on whether you use fresh-pressed cider. Strain into a chilled cocktail glass. Finish with the 2 dashes of gin and garnish with the apple slice.

HARVEST PUNCH

People are often surprised to discover that Texas has an apple season. Although it may not be a mainstay of the fall harvest as it is in New York or the Pacific Northwest, there is nonetheless a fleeting time each year when local apples and pears are available. If you are fortunate enough to have apple vendors at your local farmers' market, many of them make a fresh-pressed, unpasteurized apple cider that is well worth the money and will change the way you think about "apple juice." Mixed with local spirits, it is the base for a fabulous harvest punch.

1½ ounces Treaty Oak rum
1½ ounces fresh-pressed apple cider
½ ounce freshly squeezed lime juice
1 bar spoon Simple Syrup *(page 83)*
Dash of St. Elizabeth Allspice Dram
Dash of blackstrap or other dark rum
Ground cinnamon or freshly grated nutmeg, for garnish
Apple, lemon, and/or lime slice, for garnish *(see Note)*

Shake all the ingredients, except the garnishes, vigorously with ice to chill. Adjust the amount of syrup depending on how sweet your cider is. Strain into an ice-filled rocks glass. Dust with the cinnamon and garnish with the apple slice.

If you're making punch for a group, simply multiply the recipe by the number of people and serve in a punch bowl with a large block of ice. Dust with the cinnamon or nutmeg and garnish with apple, lemon, and/or lime slices.

Note: *When using apples or pears as a garnish, brush the cut surface of the fruit with lemon or lime juice to help prevent browning.*

GREEN HOUR

In fin de siècle Paris, the equivalent of our modern-day happy hour was known as *l' heure verte* (literally, "the green hour"; it has been noted that this "hour" problematically stretched often into many, many hours for some of its adherents). There is something romantic about the thought of absinthe being consumed on such a widespread cultural level. Unlike our European (especially Mediterranean) counterparts, Americans seem to have lost the taste for anise, though here is a contemporary cocktail that celebrates it.

1½ ounces gin	In a mixing glass, combine the gin, absinthe, lemon juice, rosemary syrup, and egg white. Shake vigorously with ice to chill and fully emulsify. Strain into a chilled cocktail glass. Garnish with a mist of Angostura bitters, swirled in the glass.
½ ounce traditional verte absinthe	
¾ ounce freshly squeezed lemon juice	
½ ounce Rosemary Syrup *(page 124)*	
1 egg white	
Angostura bitters *(use an atomizer, if available)*	

INDOCHINE STINGER

The classic Stinger consists of cognac and white crème de menthe, shaken vigorously and served over crushed ice. It's a delicious breath mint after a heavy meal, but can be cloying if you're not careful. This Stinger variation fuses Canton, a cognac-ginger liqueur, with heady, herbal Fernet.

1 ounce Domaine de Canton ginger liqueur	Combine the ingredients in a mixing glass and shake vigorously with ice to chill. Strain onto crushed ice in a chilled rocks glass.
1 ounce Fernet Branca	

GREEN HOUR

MAZATLAN

This tequila Manhattan variation comes from Paul Grosso, the other half of the Paula-Paul duo behind Paula's Texas Orange (page 42). It is essentially a Perfect Manhattan, made with *añejo* tequila with a bit of orange liqueur, which was a not uncommon component in early Manhattan recipes.

1½ ounces añejo tequila

½ ounce Paula's Texas Orange

½ ounce dry vermouth

½ ounce sweet vermouth

2 dashes of Angostura bitters

Orange twist, for garnish

Real maraschino cherry, for garnish

Stir all the ingredients, except the garnishes, in a mixing glass with ice to chill. Strain into a chilled cocktail glass. Garnish with the orange twist and maraschino cherry.

JUSTIN BAILEY

San Antonio bartender Matty Gee envisioned this cocktail to be a summer Old Fashioned variation utilizing the crisp qualities of gin rather than a whiskey. The rhubarb bitters are sweetened with a capful of Sprite and a sugar cube. Although Matty took the name as a play on the classic Major Bailey cocktail, Justin Bailey has its roots in less adult pleasures. "Justin Bailey was the power-up code to the video game Metroid," Matty explains. "Once entered, one would be provided with all power-ups and weapons. The large-format ice in this cocktail is my version of the plasma ball that would be fired to stop the space pirates from acquiring planet Zebes."

1 sugar cube
2 dashes of rhubarb bitters
½ ounce Sprite
2¼ ounces gin
Grapefruit twist, for garnish

In the bottom of a chilled Old Fashioned glass, muddle the sugar cube with the rhubarb bitters and Sprite. Add the gin and stir with a few cubes of large ice to chill. Garnish with the grapefruit twist.

MANHATTAN

The Manhattan is a classic drink that came to prominence in New York City in the closing decades of the 1800s. It is properly made with rye whiskey, though in the South it is often made with bourbon, and in Wisconsin, with brandy. Either way the cocktail requires a healthy dose of sweet vermouth and a few dashes of bitters. As with all spirits-only cocktails, it is traditional to stir and not shake this drink. There are two commonly accepted garnishes, the lemon twist and the cherry.

2 ounces 100-proof rye whiskey

1 ounce sweet vermouth

2 dashes of Angostura bitters

Real maraschino cherry or lemon twist, for garnish

Stir the whiskey, vermouth, and bitters in a mixing glass with ice and strain into a chilled cocktail glass. Garnish with the maraschino cherry or lemon twist.

COMMON MANHATTAN VARIATIONS

Dry Manhattan

Substitute dry vermouth for sweet, garnish with a lemon peel.

Perfect Manhattan

Substitute ½ ounce of dry vermouth and ½ ounce of sweet vermouth for the original 1 ounce of sweet vermouth; garnish with a lemon twist.

Jerry Thomas's Manhattan

Use 1½ ounces of rye, 1½ ounces of sweet vermouth, a bar spoon of Grand Marnier, and 3 dashes of house bitters; garnish with a lemon twist.

Rob Roy

Substitute blended scotch whiskey for the rye whiskey.

MARK McDAVID

RANGER CREEK BREWING
AND DISTILLING

Mark McDavid grew up in a military family that moved frequently during his childhood. The last move brought him to Texas, where he graduated from high school, and he decided to root his identity here by enrolling at Texas A&M University. "I was not one of those UT-hating Aggies, however," he cautions. "I played in a rock band, so we spent a lot of time in Austin." McDavid graduated with a unique education—a business degree in marketing and the equivalent of a minor in music. He put the two to good use managing the band the Sly Letter, in which he played guitar and mandolin. "'Sly Letter' was a terrible name, in retrospect," the marketing expert ruminated, "but we gained a moderate level of regional success as a touring group around Texas, and had a shot at touring with some bigger national acts."

After graduation, as the one-man marketing department for an independent family auto parts firm, he learned hands-on the ins and outs of managing and marketing a small business. After earning an MBA at UT

Austin, he was recruited to San Antonio, where he would meet his future business partners, TJ Miller and Dennis Rylander.

The Ranger Creek brewery and distillery started with a casual interest in craft brewing. "We realized that, in a way, craft brewing was basically propping up commercial brewing. It was the big thing," McDavid recalled. "But here we were in San Antonio, the seventh-biggest U.S. city, where there was a huge demand from locals and tourists alike for craft beer, and little in the way of craft brewing to satisfy the demand." They began studying home-brewing techniques in earnest and immersed themselves in their beer education, traveling far and wide to attend conferences and seminars, and no doubt drinking their fair share of beer, "But with a purpose," he insists.

In researching craft brewing, they also learned about craft distillation and hatched a plan for what would become the first brewery-distillery in Texas (and one of only a few in the country). "We wrote a ninety-nine-page business plan," McDavid explained, "which makes it a lot more comfortable for a potential investor to write a check. Even if they didn't read it, it made a thud when it hit the table." After navigating the complex web of local, state, and federal regulations, the partners began installing their new "brew-stillery" in the summer of 2010 in San Antonio. By November, their first keg of beer, the Oatmeal Pale Ale, rolled off the line.

A year later, they were bottling bourbon distilled from grain that was mashed at their own facility and aged in small oak barrels in a rackhouse on the premises. Because every drop of whiskey sold under the Ranger Creek label is mashed, distilled, and aged at their facility, McDavid takes issue with so-called local whiskeys that are distilled elsewhere in the United States and brought to Texas in barrels.

"The consumer has a right to know whether a bottle marked 'Texas whiskey' actually contains whiskey distilled in Texas. Calling something that was distilled in Kentucky 'Texas whiskey' is misleading."

He believes that the pertinent information should be available. "Distilled versus rectified vodka, distilled versus blended and bottled bourbon—which one is better or worse is for consumers to decide, but they have to know what they're buying."

As for the future of Ranger Creek, McDavid says, "We're sticking to whiskey, especially distilling our beers into whiskeys. We built our facility for flexibility, so we could theoretically do something else, but our business model is based on the intersection between beer and whiskey. We've got so many whiskeys we want to make right now that it will take a long time to run out of ideas." ☙

CLASSIC DRY MARTINI

According to "research mixologist" Robert Hess, the perfect calibration for the Classic Dry Martini is that point at which you cease to taste where the vermouth stops and the gin begins—in other words, where the two ingredients achieve perfect harmony. This ratio is different not just for every drinker, but also for every set of ingredients, as vermouths and gins are as varied as Martini drinkers' palates. Start with this as a guideline, but try a variety of ratios until you find what is perfectly in balance for your own palate. Note that the Classic Dry Martini is stirred, as is the convention any time a drink consists only of spiritous ingredients. This is never more important than with the Martini—a stirred Martini is viscous, boozy, and impeccably clear, like a gemstone in the glass. By contrast, a shaken Martini is thin, watery, and cloudy to the eye.

2½ ounces gin
½ ounce dry vermouth
3 drops orange bitters *(optional)*
Lemon twist or olive, for garnish

Combine the gin, vermouth, and bitters in a mixing glass. Stir with ice to chill, then strain into a chilled cocktail glass. Garnish with the lemon twist or olive.

> *"Then comes the zenith of man's pleasure.*
> *Then comes the julep—the mint julep.*
> *Who has not tasted one has lived in vain."*
>
> —Joshua Soule Smith, Kentucky colonel *(Lexington Herald, 1880s)*

MINT JULEP

There is no cocktail more likely to inspire the passions of a Southerner than the Mint Julep. Although the julep category predates the modern cocktail and included a number of permutations, the formula is now generally agreed upon. The official drink of the Kentucky Derby, every Kentuckian has his or her own recipe, which by necessity means that every other recipe is wrong, or at least inferior. Some serve the cocktail with the mint in the glass; some call that an abomination. Some make a mint syrup; some muddle. Some serve the drink with straws, whereas others would rather kill kittens than sip a Mint Julep that way. Beyond the debate over technique, this much can be agreed upon: There are only four ingredients in the classic Mint Julep—bourbon, mint, sugar, and ice. If you see lime or soda or anything else, you may channel your inner Southerner and become rightfully indignant.

MINT JULEP

2 sprigs fresh mint

2 ounces bourbon

¼ to ½ ounce Simple Syrup *(page 83)*

Powdered sugar *(optional)*

Using a muddler, gently bruise one of the mint sprigs in the bottom and up the sides of a julep cup (see Note); discard. Add 1 ounce of the bourbon and fill the cup with crushed ice. Stir until the cup is frosty. Add the remaining ounce of bourbon to the cup and fill again with crushed ice. Pour the simple syrup over the top and stir until frosty. Adjust the syrup to taste. Top again with crushed ice. Spank the remaining sprig of mint and place in the cup. Some partisans prefer to dust the top of the julep and the mint sprig with powdered sugar to amplify the "frosted" effect.

JULEP CUP

These small pewter, silver-plated, or sterling silver cups are a staple of the Southern sideboard. Often monogrammed and given as gifts to signify special occasions such as anniversaries and graduations, the julep cup's most noble duty is as vessel for the julep itself. The metal acts as a conductor, and the cup frosts up as heat is drawn out of the whiskey and the julep cools. Of course, a julep in the "wrong" glass is better than no julep at all, so don't despair if you are fresh out of julep cups. At the Kentucky Derby itself, in fact, the drink is served in a tall, thin, Collins-type glass. (You can order the official glasses online from the Derby Store if you want to add a touch of Churchill Downs to your next Derby Day Party.) A highball or double Old Fashioned glass is perfectly suitable for making Mint Juleps at home.

Note: *In my experience, rare is the occasion that I make only one julep. For occasions that involve Mint Juleps in quantity, I recommend making a mint syrup (see Herb Syrups, page 124).*

OLD FREDERICKSBURG JULEP

Highway 290 leading southwest from Austin used to be known as the Fredericksburg Highway. Although mostly gone now, sections of that old thoroughfare pop up here and there as Old Fredericksburg Road. This cocktail is a nod to the famous fruits that await travelers at the end of that road, in Texas's "peach belt" around Stonewall and Fredericksburg.

2 sprigs fresh mint

2 ounces bourbon

½ ounce Peach Syrup *(see Note)*

Using a muddler, gently bruise one of the mint sprigs in the bottom and up the sides of a julep cup; discard. Add 1 ounce of the bourbon and fill the cup with crushed ice. Stir until the cup is frosty. Add the remaining ounce of bourbon to the cup and fill again with crushed ice. Pour the peach syrup over the top and stir until frosty. Top again with crushed ice. "Spank" the remaining mint sprig to release its aroma, and place in the cup.

Note: *Peach syrup can be accomplished one of several ways. If you have a pulp extractor–style juicer, juice peaches and bring equal parts peach juice and sugar to just enough of a simmer to dissolve the sugar without compromising the fresh peach flavor. You can also bring two parts peeled, pitted, and diced peaches, one part sugar, and one part water to a simmer in a saucepan until the peaches begin to dissolve and a prominent peach flavor reveals itself. Strain out any solids. Taste the syrup and adjust for sweetness. As a last resort, use store-bought peach nectar, which will already have some sweetness added. Bring equal parts of peach nectar and sugar to a simmer. Stir until dissolved. Bottle and store refrigerated for up to 1 month.*

ORCHARD JULEP

Alba Huerta began her bartending career at Houston's Timberwolf Pub, a neighborhood bar where she learned the incredible extent to which family and friends can form around a drinking establishment. While studying business at UNLV, she also got an education of a different sort, working in the fiercely competitive food and beverage industry of Las Vegas. Back in Houston she eventually made her way to Anvil Bar & Refuge, a bar and team that is changing the landscape of Houston's Westheimer Boulevard and that helped put Texas on the cocktail map. Her bar in Houston is named, fittingly, Julep.

6 to 8 fresh mint leaves, plus 1 sprig for garnish

1 bar spoon Raw Sugar Syrup *(page 135)*

1 ounce Kina l'Avion d'Or

½ ounce applejack

½ ounce Daron Calvados

Dash of Angostura bitters

Powdered sugar

Combine the mint leaves and the syrup in the bottom of a julep cup and muddle gently. Add the kina, applejack, calvados, and bitters. Fill three-quarters of the cup with crushed ice and stir for ten revolutions. Fill with crushed ice to the top of the cup, being sure to create a mound of ice on top. Garnish with the mint sprig and sprinkle with the powdered sugar.

KINA

Kina or quinquina is a class of aperitif wines that dates to the middle of the nineteenth century. It takes its name from quinine, a bittering agent derived from the bark of the cinchona tree, which was once used widely as an antimalarial agent. The wines were sweetened and flavored with herbs and spices to make the bitter quinine more palatable. Eventually quinquinas became used for more recreational purposes. The most famous of the kinas was Kina Lillet, an essential component of James Bond's Vesper Martini. Unfortunately over time, Kina Lillet was reformulated and lost the "Kina" from its name. Its tamer version is now known only as Lillet—a perfectly quaffable aperitif wine, albeit not a quinquina. Their Italian counterparts are known as chinati, of which Cocchi Americano is an example.

CALVADOS AND APPLEJACK

Calvados is a French brandy distilled from cider made of apples (also pears) in a region designated by that spirit's Appellation d'Origine Contrôlée (AOC), or controlled designation of origin. A rustic cousin to calvados is applejack, a domestic American spirit, arguably the oldest distilled spirit in the United States—the first licensed distillery in the country was Laird's, an applejack producer still in business today. Applejack takes its name from a historical process known as jacking, by which the alcohol content of fermented cider was concentrated by freezing the liquid and removing ice as the cider froze. In contrast with distilled spirits, there was little in the way of quality control using this method. Over time applejack became a distilled spirit, and much of today's applejack is not made entirely from fermented apples, but a blend of apple brandy and grain spirits, due to the comparably higher cost of distilling spirits from fruit. By law as well as by tradition, calvados is distilled entirely from apples and pears.

NEGRONI

The Negroni is a turn-of-the-century evolution of the Americano Cocktail, a cocktail made with Campari and sweet vermouth topped with club soda. When gin was added and soda was removed, the great classic Negroni was born, and it remains one of the most enduring of cocktails from the time period. In Italy it is served on the rocks, which is my preference; in the United States, the Negroni is often served straight up. As is traditional with Campari cocktails, it is garnished with an orange peel.

1 ounce gin
1 ounce Campari
1 ounce sweet vermouth
Orange peel, for garnish

Combine the gin, Campari, and sweet vermouth in a mixing glass with ice and stir to chill. Strain over fresh ice in an Old Fashioned glass, or into a chilled cocktail glass. Garnish with the orange peel.

NEGRONI VARIATIONS

The Negroni is such a timeless formula, it has been the foundation for numerous variations, both historically and in the present.

Old Pal
Substitute rye whiskey for the gin, dry vermouth for the sweet vermouth.

Boulevardier
Substitute bourbon for the gin.

MAZ CHINGONI

The Chingoni was a cocktail developed by San Antonio bartender Jeret Peña and myself when we were working on the restoration and reopening of the historic Esquire Tavern. It was made with aged gin, Aperol, and the super-vermouth Carpano Antica. If you understand Spanish, the name implies, essentially, that this was a super bad-ass Negroni variant. Jeret has now made it even more *chingón* by making it with tequila and lacing it with mezcal.

¾ ounce añejo tequila
¾ ounce Aperol
¾ ounce sweet vermouth
¼ ounce mezcal
Grapefruit peel, for garnish

Combine the tequila, Aperol, sweet vermouth, and mezcal in a mixing glass with ice and stir to chill. Strain over a large chunk of fresh ice in an Old Fashioned glass. Garnish with the grapefruit peel.

OLD FASHIONED

The Old Fashioned, apropos of its name, is one of the oldest cocktails in the book. That is, it is based on the formula of what we understand to be the original definition of *cocktail*, which was described in a turn-of-the-nineteenth-century newspaper as a drink consisting of a base spirit seasoned with bitters, sweetened with sugar, and tempered with water. Therefore, if you ordered a "whiskey cocktail," you would likely receive a glass of whiskey treated in the manner prescribed above. *Cocktail* implied the mixed drink conformed to a specific formula.

Over time, as the trade of bartending expanded, so did the practitioner's repertoire, and along with it the very definition of *cocktail*. A late-nineteenth-century drinker who ordered a "whiskey cocktail" would be confronted with myriad available options, noteworthy among them the Manhattan. *Cocktail* no longer referred to a single type of drink, but to a broad category of drinks. (Eventually the term's meaning would evolve such that it no longer required alcohol at all, as evidenced by such "cocktails" as shrimp, fruit, and Molotov.) If a customer preferred that earlier, simpler type of cocktail, he could specify that he wanted an "old-fashioned" whiskey cocktail. By the time the first cocktail manuals were printed in the 1860s and '70s, this change had already taken place, and eventually the name of the original drink was truncated to "Old Fashioned," which is how it is known today.

While the name endures, what is not the same is the preparation, with two distinct methods diverging over time. The most common today is the muddled version, in which an orange slice and a maraschino cherry are muddled in the bottom of the glass with sugar and bitters.

Although it is the method most contemporary bartenders are familiar with, the muddled version is an invention of the twentieth century. The old Old Fashioned cocktail would have been garnished with an expressed lemon or orange peel (I prefer both) but not the fruit's flesh, and no cherry. It is one of those variations that has been around long enough to attain its own legitimacy, and so both versions are included here. When making an Old Fashioned for someone else, it is appropriate to ask how the imbiber prefers it.

MUDDLED OLD FASHIONED

CLASSIC OLD FASHIONED

CLASSIC OLD FASHIONED

This version utilizes citrus zest as opposed to whole fruit, and is akin to what might have constituted an "original" Old Fashioned (minus the ice, of course, which was in scarce and in only seasonal supply in the early 1800s).

1 sugar cube, or ¼ to ½ ounce Simple Syrup *(page 83)*

A few drops of water

Lemon

Orange

2 ounces 100-proof rye whiskey

3 dashes of aromatic bitters, such as Angostura

In the bottom of an Old Fashioned glass, muddle the sugar cube with the tiniest amount of water necessary to render it into a rustic syrup. Alternatively, use simple syrup to taste. Using a swivel-handled vegetable peeler, remove a strip of lemon peel and a strip of orange peel from the respective fruits over the glass, allowing the peels to fall into the glass and capturing as much essential oil as possible. Add the whiskey and bitters. Fill the glass with ice, preferably in large chunks. Stir using a bar spoon to integrate and dilute. No additional garnish is needed.

Note: *The drink should be stirred, not shaken. It is traditionally made with a muddled sugar cube, though simple syrup is acceptable (superfine or "caster" sugar is also an option, though powdered sugar is not). The original drink would have been made with rye whiskey, which I recommend. Regional variations exist—in the South, bourbon is used; in parts of the Midwest, it is not uncommon to see a Brandy Old Fashioned.*

MUDDLED OLD FASHIONED

The Old Fashioned underwent a design change in the twentieth century, when it became common practice to muddle an orange wedge and cherry in the bottom of the glass.

Orange wedge

Real maraschino cherry

1 sugar cube, or ¼ to ½ ounce Simple Syrup *(page 83)*

2 ounces 100-proof rye whiskey

3 dashes of aromatic bitters, such as Angostura

In the bottom of an Old Fashioned glass, muddle the orange wedge, maraschino cherry, and sugar or syrup to taste. Add the whiskey and bitters. Fill the glass with ice, preferably in large chunks. Stir using a bar spoon to integrate and dilute.

OLD AUSTIN

This Old Fashioned variation was created by well-known Austin cocktail bartender Bill Norris to capture the flavor of Austin's rowdier frontier days.

Lemon

Orange

½ ounce Pecan Syrup *(recipe follows)*

2 dashes of whiskey barrel–aged bitters or Angostura bitters

2 ounces 100-proof rye whiskey

Using a swivel-handled vegetable peeler, remove a strip of lemon peel and a strip of orange peel from the respective fruits over an Old Fashioned glass, allowing the peels to fall into the glass and capturing as much essential oil as possible. Add the pecan syrup, bitters, and whiskey. Fill the glass with ice, preferably in large chunks, and stir using a bar spoon to integrate and dilute.

PECAN SYRUP

Makes about 2 cups

1 cup refined or raw sugar

1 cup filtered water

½ cup raw pecan halves

Combine the sugar and water in a small saucepan and place over medium-high heat. Rough-chop the pecan halves and add them to the sugar mixture once it has come to a simmer. Simmer for 10 minutes, then remove from the heat and allow to cool for 2 minutes. Strain out the pecans pieces and allow the syrup to cool. Store refrigerated for up to 1 month.

DRY CREEK OLD FASHIONED

This cocktail was created by my friends Lara Nixon and Jason Stevens for the launch of Bad Dog, the first bitters company in Texas. The cocktail is an Old Fashioned variation made entirely from Texas ingredients.

1 sugar cube

4 dashes of Bad Dog Barcraft Sarsaparilla Dry Bitters

½ ounce carbonated water *(or regular water)*

1½ ounces Balcones Rumble

Texas red grapefruit *(look for a nice firm fruit)*

Place the sugar cube in the bottom of an Old Fashioned glass. Add the bitters and carbonated water, and muddle the sugar into a simple syrup solution. Add the Balcones Rumble. Over this glass, peel a nice-size strip of grapefruit rind (it is very important to do this over the glass to capture all of the expressed oils). Twist the peel and drop it into the glass. Add a couple of ice cubes and stir for a good 15 seconds. Top with more ice.

PECANS

The pecan has been the State Tree of Texas since 1919, though it has been part of our culinary tradition for much longer. Unlike many of the agricultural products that are identified with Texas, pecans are actually native to the state. Archaeological evidence suggests that pecans, which grow only in North America, originated from the area around the Rio Grande valley along what is now the Texas-Mexico border. Native Americans carried the nuts with them as they migrated throughout Texas and the Southeast, planting the trees along waterways to ensure a perennial source of food as they and their ancestors returned in ensuing years.

By the turn of the nineteenth century, pecans were being cultivated all across the southeastern United States, though Texas made particularly big business out of the commercialization of our native nut. Today, Texas reigns as a top pecan-producing state in the country (occasionally alternating with New Mexico and Georgia for the top spot).

MATT'S OLD FASHIONED

For generations of Austinites, dining at Matt's El Rancho has been a tradition that has often begun in utero. This tequila Old Fashioned variation is a tribute to that venerable temple of Tex-Mex.

Lemon

Orange

2 ounces añejo tequila

½ ounce St-Germain elderflower liqueur

2 dashes of Angostura bitters

Dash of orange bitters

Using a swivel-handled vegetable peeler, remove a strip of lemon peel and a strip of orange peel from the respective fruits over an Old Fashioned glass, allowing the peels to fall into the glass and capturing as much essential oil as possible. Add the tequila, St-Germain, and both bitters. Fill the glass with ice, preferably in large chunks. Stir using a bar spoon to integrate and dilute.

OLD SMOKEY

Anybody who grew up in Texas very likely had an Old Smokey charcoal grill in the backyard, or at least had a neighbor who had one. These utilitarian beauties have been made by a Houston-based company since the 1920s, and, amazingly, are still manufactured in Texas. This cocktail gets its name from that recreational staple, but gets its smoky flavor from artisanal mezcal.

Lemon

Orange

1 ounce añejo tequila

1 ounce mezcal *(see page 170)*

¼ ounce amber agave nectar

2 dashes of Angostura bitters

Using a swivel-handled vegetable peeler, remove a strip of lemon peel and a strip of orange peel from the respective fruits over an Old Fashioned glass, allowing the peels to fall into the glass and capturing as much essential oil as possible. Add the tequila, mezcal, agave nectar, and bitters. Adjust the agave nectar to taste. Fill the glass with ice, preferably in large chunks. Stir using a bar spoon to integrate and dilute.

MEZCAL

Although it is gaining a measure of prominence in respectable cocktail establishments, for many drinkers the mention of mezcal conjures up memories of a rough night in a border town, swilling rustic hooch from a bottle that most likely had a worm swimming in the bottom. Such an evening may or may not have involved a transaction with a member of the local adult entertainment workforce, but it no doubt resulted in a hangover of Hollywood proportions. The problem with this scenario is not mezcal itself, but poor-quality mezcal, overconsumed. These lower-quality, industrial *mezcales* do exist and are worthy of derision. Mezcal at its finest is an otherworldly drinking experience, a truly artisanal product, made using heritage methods that seem anachronistic by comparison to mezcal's more familiar relation, tequila.

The epicenter of mezcal production is in the Mexican state of Oaxaca. A look at mezcal production offers a glimpse into what tequila production would have looked like before that process became industrialized over the latter half of the twentieth century. Mezcal is the parent category of which tequila is a specific type—in other words, all tequila is mezcal, though not all mezcal is tequila.

There are several important distinctions to note between these two spirits. First, whereas tequila may only be made from one species of agave, the Weber Blue variety, there are a number of different agaves—many of them wild—that can be used to make mezcal, with each imparting its unique qualities into the spirit.

Second, mezcal is still produced largely by hand in very small distilleries known as *palenques*. Most steps of the process are powered by humans or beasts of burden. Harvested agaves are brought to the *palenque* where they are roasted in a traditional earthen oven—a large conical pit lined with volcanic rocks that become white hot from a fire lit beneath. Once hot, the stones are covered with a layer of spent agave fibers known as bagasse, from previous distillation. The bagasse creates a protective barrier between the hot rocks and raw agaves and also releases steam once heated, aiding in the roasting process. Agaves are piled on top and covered with a tarp that is then covered by dirt. The agaves will roast in this earthen oven for several days.

Once roasted, the agaves are milled using a traditional *tahona*, a large round stone that is pulled by a horse or donkey around a circular pit where the agaves are crushed. Crushed agave fibers and the resulting honeylike juices are transferred to a fermentation tank, where they will combine with water and wild yeast to create fermented, low-alcohol *mosto*. The *mosto* is distilled twice in a traditional still made of copper or stainless steel (sometimes clay), and the resulting liquid is mezcal.

The variety of agaves used and the traditional production practices employed result in a tremendously diverse flavor profile across the numerous mezcal producers, creating a much wider spectrum than for tequila.

PREFECT

As a product of Texas's public schools, I have always been intrigued by old-guard East Coast prep schools and colleges. Many of the latter have their own cocktails, such as the Harvard, the Princeton, and the Yale. The Prefect is a tribute to my fantasy of what I would drink if I went to an Ivy League school, though I imagine most preppies are drinking Keystone Light like college kids everywhere else.

1½ ounces 100-proof rye whiskey

¾ ounce ruby port

½ ounce Averna Amaro

1 bar spoon crème de cassis

Dash of Fee Brothers Whiskey Barrel–Aged Bitters or Angostura bitters

Real maraschino cherry, for garnish

Stir all the ingredients except the cherry in a mixing glass with ice to chill. Strain into a chilled cocktail glass and garnish with the maraschino cherry.

RED RAIDER

Bourbon, apple, and preserved cherry are some of my favorite flavors for fall cocktails, such as this lightly spiced whiskey sour.

½ small red apple, such as Gala, peeled, cored, and diced into large chunks

2 Luxardo original Marasca cherries or house-preserved cherries

1 bar spoon syrup from cherries

2 ounces bourbon (preferably Maker's Mark 46)

¾ ounce freshly squeezed lemon juice

1 bar spoon Simple Syrup (page 83)

Dash of Bitter Truth Creole Bitters or Peychaud's Bitters

Thin apple slice, for garnish

In the bottom of a mixing glass, muddle the apple chunks, cherries, and cherry syrup. Add the bourbon, lemon juice, simple syrup, and bitters and shake vigorously with ice to chill. Strain into a chilled cocktail glass and garnish with the apple slice.

MARASCHINO CHERRIES

The "maraschino cherry" familiar to most modern drinkers bears little resemblance to its namesake, the small, sour Marasca cherry grown in Croatia and northern Italy. The clear liqueur known as maraschino (pronounced with a hard *k* sound) is made from the cherries as well as their pits. As opposed to a cherry liqueur, maraschino is distilled from the whole fruit, with the pits imparting a bitter almond–like flavor to the dry, aromatic, complex, funky spirit. Maraschino was a common sweetener in a number of classic late-nineteenth-century cocktails such as the Martinez and early versions of the Manhattan. Cherries preserved and packed in the liqueur took on its name. In the United States, a different process emerged, though the cherries kept the maraschino name: Local cherries such as Queen Anne are put through a brining process whereby the color is removed, after which point the cherries are sweetened and treated with artificial color and additional flavorings. Fortunately for the modern drinker, traditional Luxardo Marasca cherries are becoming more widely available; when you taste these rich, dense gems next to the cherry from your sundae, the latter pales in comparison. Although they are comparatively costly, real Marasca maraschino cherries are an affordable luxury when you consider how few cherries you use, and how vastly superior the real ones are to the artificial variety.

DAN GARRISON

GARRISON BROTHERS
DISTILLING

If you've ever met Dan Garrison, it's hard to imagine this man working on Madison Avenue. With a cowboy hat and goatee, he looks more like a small-town sheriff than an adman, and is a Texan through and through. As a child, Garrison moved all around his home state, eventually graduating from high school in Dallas. He moved to Austin to go to UT, graduating with a BS in communications. But BS is something he doesn't countenance, as anyone who has ever met him or tried his whiskey can attest.

After college he moved to New York and worked for major advertising agencies, selling everything from children's cereal to motor oil. His main accomplishment in the Big Apple, however, was meeting his future wife. Fortunately for him, she is a five-generation native Austinite, and together they moved back home. After working for a major local advertising firm, Garrison did what so many Austin entrepreneurs did in the 1990s and went to work for a high-tech start-up. When the tech bubble burst, so did the value of his equity shares, and he realized it was time for a change.

Garrison saw the emergence of the small distilling movement as his opportunity and began making research missions to Kentucky, where he met such titans of the bourbon trade as Harlan Wheatley and Elmer Lee. In 2007 he obtained his distiller's permit, bought a still, and located it on a 16-acre parcel of ranch land outside the Hill Country town of Hye. In 2008 he laid down the first barrels of Texas bourbon.

Of course, bourbon ages differently in the hills of Texas than in the hills of Kentucky. In the extreme Texas heat, distillers might see an "angel's share"— the portion lost to evaporation—as high as 10 to 12 percent annually, whereas that figure might be 3 to 5 percent in Kentucky. The climate conditions combined with the smaller barrels employed at Garrison Brothers results in a whiskey that matures more quickly than does whiskey aged in larger barrels in cooler climes. (The use of small barrels is not without controversy—especially if you ask the established big distillers!) Garrison released his first straight bourbon—one that is at least two years old—in 2010.

Considering Dan Garrison used to peddle in hype, he's pretty short on it these days. He has no plans to expand outside of Texas, or into other spirit categories. "Straight bourbon is sexy," he says. "The pool is wide and deep— you can make so many variations and still stay inside the category." Garrison is selling a Texas whiskey for Texas consumers. "When people think of Texas whiskey, I want them to ask about the quality, and where the whiskey came from." He won't name names, but points out that a number of whiskey bottlers don't make their own juice. "When you buy Texas wine, it is guaranteed by law to contain at least 75 percent Texas grapes, but there are no such guarantees with Texas whiskey."

There is no secret as to where the whiskey comes from at Garrison Brothers. The distillery is located conveniently near one end of the Texas Wine Trail and receives thousands of visitors a year. "Giving tours is the best advertising for us," Garrison says. "You get to see and taste every step in the process, and gain an understanding of why it costs what it does." And because Texas law does not allow distilleries to sell their own product, Garrison was lucky enough that a couple of area ranchers opened a liquor store just down the road from him. ❧

SAZERAC

The Sazerac dates back to the middle decades of the nineteenth century and is one of the oldest, most continually drunk cocktails in the United States. It hails from New Orleans, and even became the Official Cocktail of that town in 2008. (Not surprisingly, New Orleans was the first American city to seek and obtain such a designation.) Originally the drink was made with cognac, but by the end of the 1800s, it was primarily a rye whiskey drink. Today in New Orleans you can have it either way, or if you can't decide, split the difference.

2 ounces 100-proof rye whiskey or cognac

¼ to ½ ounce Simple Syrup *(page 83)*, **or 1 or 2 sugar cubes**

6 dashes of Peychaud's Bitters

Herbsaint or absinthe

Lemon "coin," for garnish

Combine the whiskey, simple syrup, and bitters in a mixing glass with ice. (If using sugar cubes, muddle the sugar and bitters and the smallest amount of water if necessary to create a syrup, then add the whiskey.) Stir to chill, and adjust the syrup to taste. Rinse an Old Fashioned glass with the Herbsaint and discard the Herbsaint. Strain the cocktail into the absinthe-rinsed glass. Flame the lemon "coin" over the glass and discard.

SIDECAR

Born in the Prohibition era, the Sidecar is one of the great classic "gateway" cocktails—a perfect way to segue a Margarita drinker to something a little more adventurous. It is a drink on the dry side, though a sugared rim is a classic treatment for this cocktail.

1½ ounces cognac or brandy
1 ounce Cointreau
¾ ounce freshly squeezed lemon juice
Orange zest, for garnish

Combine the cognac, Cointreau, and lemon juice in a mixing glass and shake vigorously with ice to chill. Strain into a chilled cocktail glass with a sugared rim. Garnish with the orange zest.

SIDECAR VARIATIONS 🍸

If the Sidecar itself is a variation on a Brandy Daisy or Crusta, then the drink also lends itself easily to improvisation. Here are a couple:

CABLE CAR

Tony Abou-Ganim's legendary—and legendarily easy-sipping—Sidecar variation simply substitutes spiced rum for the cognac and adds a little cinnamon spice to the rim. It was created in the 1990s for the opening of Harry Denton's Starlight Room in San Francisco.

1½ ounces spiced rum

¾ ounce Cointreau or Paula's Texas Orange

1 ounce freshly squeezed lemon juice

½ ounce Simple Syrup (page 83)

Cinnamon-sugar

Combine all the liquid ingredients in a mixing glass and shake vigorously with ice to chill. Strain into a chilled cocktail glass that has been rimmed with cinnamon-sugar (see Technique Tip: Glass Rimming, page 130).

STREETCAR NAMED DESIRE

For a special showing of the papers of Tennessee Williams, I took inspiration from Tony's Cable Car and added absinthe, in honor of that other famous American city with streetcars.

1½ ounces spiced rum

1 ounce Cointreau or Paula's Texas Orange

½ ounce Tenneyson Absinthe Royale or other blanche absinthe

¾ ounce freshly squeezed lemon juice

1 bar spoon Simple Syrup (page 83)

Orange zest, for garnish

Combine all the ingredients, except the orange peel, in a mixing glass and shake vigorously with ice to chill. Strain into a chilled cocktail glass and garnish with the expressed orange zest.

THE BRAVE 🍷

"In Texas and across the South you see bolder cuisines, bolder flavors, and Southern diners have bolder palates," explains Houston native and Anvil bartender Bobby Heugel. "At Anvil we definitely have a bolder style, and The Brave is our house cocktail. It's served at room temperature, which challenges many people's basic precepts about cocktails, but the Averna tones down the intensity of the drink. There are so many different factors that you can change when creating a cocktail. I worked on this for about a year, trying numerous flavor combinations before arriving at the final version." Heugel says the last element to fall into place was the glass. "The Brave is served in a wineglass. When I put it in the wineglass, I knew I had the finishing touch."

1 ounce Del Maguey Chichicapa Mezcal

1 ounce Hacienda de Chihuahua Sotol Plata

½ ounce Averna Amaro

1 bar spoon Grand Marnier or orange curaçao

3 mists of Angostura bitters *(use an atomizer)*

Flamed orange zest, for garnish

Pour the first four ingredients into a Bordeaux-style wineglass and swirl to combine. Spritz the interior of the glass and surface of the drink with 3 mists of Angostura bitters. Garnish with the flamed orange zest.

TEXECUTIONER

This cocktail by Austin bartender Houston Eaves will assault the palate with a trio of far-out flavors that combine for harmonious effect. D'Aristi is a Mexican liqueur with Mayan origins, made from rum flavored with honey and anise. Cocchi Americano is a slightly bitter Italian aperitif wine—not dissimilar to vermouth—that is flavored with cinchona, gentian, citrus peel, and herbs.

¾ **ounce Espadin mezcal**

¾ **ounce D'Aristi Xtabentun**

¾ **ounce Cocchi Americano**

¾ **ounce freshly squeezed red grapefruit juice**

Wide strip of red grapefruit zest, for garnish

Combine the mezcal, D'Aristi, Cocchi Americano, and grapefruit juice in a mixing glass and shake vigorously with ice to chill. Strain into a chilled cocktail glass. Over the surface of the drink, express the oil from the grapefruit zest. Garnish with the zest.

SUFFERING BAPTIST

The Suffering Bastard is a 1940s tiki standby that was originally made with bourbon and gin as its base. This variation utilizes cask-strength True Blue corn whiskey from Balcones Distilling in Waco, with a nod to that city's famous teetotaling population.

1½ ounces Balcones True Blue Cask Strength Corn Whisky

1 ounce Plymouth Sloe Gin

1 ounce freshly squeezed lime juice

Dash of Angostura bitters

2 ounces Maine Root ginger beer

Lime wheel, for garnish

Build the liquid ingredients over crushed ice in a double Old Fashioned glass or goblet; stir or swizzle to mix. Garnish with the lime wheel.

SMOKING GYPSY

This cocktail was the winning entry from Houston Eaves in the 2011 Official Drink of Austin contest. He took his inspiration from the pre-Prohibition-era cocktail, the Gypsy, and updated it with local Texas flavors.

1¾ ounces Tito's Handmade Vodka

¾ ounce Benedictine

½ ounce Balcones Brimstone Smoked Corn Whisky

Dash of Bad Dog Smoke and Damnation Bitters

Dash of Angostura bitters

Strip of red grapefruit zest

Combine the vodka, Benedictine, whiskey, and both bitters in a mixing glass with ice and stir to chill. Strain over one large ice cube in a rocks glass. Express the oil from a strip of grapefruit zest over the drink, and garnish with the grapefruit twist.

SUFFERING BAPTIST

TEXAS MAI TAI

The Mai Tai was at one point more well known in this country than the Margarita. It originated in the tiki palaces of either Victor "Trader Vic" Bergeron or Donn "Don the Beachcomber" Beach, depending on whom you ask, but it had spread from sea to shining sea by the height of the tiki boom. As with many classically formulated cocktails, but with tropical drinks in particular, bartenders are prone to overcomplicating the simplicity of this drink. The Mai Tai is a simple concoction of rum, lime juice, orange liqueur, and orgeat, an almond syrup (see Orgeat, page 109). In less adept hands it is not uncommon to see the drink made with pineapple juice, orange juice, grenadine, and other unnecessary adulterants. Here I offer an all-Texas version that adheres to the spirit of the original drink, but can be made from entirely local ingredients (at least during that brief period when Texas limes are in season).

1 ounce Treaty Oak Platinum Rum

1 ounce Treaty Oak Antique Rum

½ ounce Paula's Texas Orange

¾ ounce Orgeat (page 109; for an extra-Texas-y Mai Tai, try pecan orgeat)

¾ ounce freshly squeezed lime juice

Fresh mint, for garnish

Lime wedge, for garnish

Combine the rums, Paula's Texas Orange, orgeat, and lime juice in a mixing glass and shake vigorously with ice to chill. Strain into an Old Fashioned glass filled with crushed ice. Garnish abundantly with the mint and the lime wedge. A sugarcane stick or orchid would be an especially extravagant touch, and extravagant touches are de rigueur with tiki drinks.

WINTER CITRUS PUNCH

Although red grapefruits are the stars of the Texas citrus crop, our winter markets are chock-full of all manner of citrus, including satsumas, Meyer lemons, Mexican limes, tangerines, and pomelos. This easy, attractive punch marries such typical winter cocktail ingredients as bourbon and ginger with aromatic rosemary and the bright zing of local citrus. *Makes approximately 30 cocktails, which should satisfy a moderately thirsty crowd of 10*

1 liter bourbon

1 cup Aperol

¾ cup Paula's Texas Lemon or other limoncello

2¼ cups freshly squeezed grapefruit juice

¾ cup freshly squeezed lemon juice

1 cup cold water

¾ to 1 cup ginger syrup

Large block of ice

A variety of citrus wheels, for garnish

Rosemary sprigs, for garnish

Combine the liquid ingredients in a punch bowl and add ice. Stir to combine and chill. Taste and adjust the ginger syrup for the sweetness to your liking. Garnish with the citrus wheels and rosemary sprigs.

Note: *If you do not have time to make ginger syrup, you could substitute a good-quality ginger beer and adjust the sweetness level by adding Simple Syrup (page 83).*

SNAIL

Cocktails of the tiki persuasion are often notorious for their prohibitive number of ingredients, some of them obscure or proprietary. With the Snail we extend that protocol to an absurd point. When developing cocktail recipes, inspiration can come from anywhere. In this case it was the snail. *Makes about 15 cocktails*

8 ounces Flor de Caña Gold Rum

4 ounces Daron Calvados

2 ounces Cruzan Blackstrap rum

2 ounces St. George Aqua Perfecta Pear Liqueur

2 ounces cachaça

2 ounces Domaine de Canton ginger liqueur

2 ounces Balcones Rumble

1¾ ounces Aperol

½ ounce Hum liqueur

2 ounces Simple Syrup *(page 83)*

4 ounces freshly squeezed lime juice

2 ounces freshly squeezed lemon juice

6 to 8 dashes of Bitter Truth Jerry Thomas's Own Decanter Bitters

Build the ingredients in a large mixing cup and transfer to a giant porcelain snail filled with big chunks of ice topped with crushed ice. Serve with colorful straws.

WOODEN SHIPS

Jason Stevens is one of Austin's top cocktail bartenders. While his talents are voluminous, it is upon the cocktail's high seas that he prefers to travel. This pirate's dram is his idea of a perfect tiki nightcap.

1 ounce plus 1 bar spoon Neisson Rhum Agricole Réserve Spéciale

Scant 1 ounce Cynar

Scant bar spoon grade B maple syrup

2 dashes of Bittermens Xocolatl Mole bitters

Combine all the ingredients in a mixing glass. Stir briefly with ice and strain onto fresh ice (preferably a few large ice cubes) in an Old Fashioned glass.

SWEET, CREAMY, AND DESSERTY

After-dinner drinks for those who prefer to take their dessert in liquid form

ABSINTHE EGGNOG

ABSINTHE EGGNOG ☕

I first discovered absinthe eggnog while attending the annual Fête de Absinthe in tiny Boveresse, Switzerland, near the French-Swiss border. It was a flavor combination so beguiling that I was immediately smitten. The prevailing absinthe in Switzerland is a clear style known as *blanche* or *la bleue*, and that is what I've recommended here. I advise trying the single cocktail first before committing to the full batch—the flavor profile of absinthe is not for everyone.

1½ ounces Tenneyson Absinthe Royale or other blanche absinthe

1½ ounces heavy cream

¾ ounce Raw Sugar Syrup *(page 135)* **or Pecan Syrup** *(page 166)*

½ teaspoon vanilla extract

1 whole egg

Combine all the ingredients in a mixing glass and shake for a moment without ice (alternatively, use a handheld milk frother to emulsify the ingredients). Add ice and shake vigorously to chill. Strain into a punch cup. You can also make this in a blender by blending all the ingredients with a scant handful of ice until thoroughly emulsified.

BATCHED COCKTAIL ☕

Makes approximately 20 cocktails

2 dozen eggs, separated

2½ cups sugar

3 cups half-and-half

3 tablespoons vanilla extract

1 (750 ml) bottle Tenneyson Absinthe Royale or other blanche absinthe

Freshly grated nutmeg, for garnish

With an electric mixer, beat the egg yolks with 2 cups of the sugar until they are light in color. Transfer to another bowl and mix in the half-and-half, vanilla, and absinthe.

Beat the egg whites separately in a clean bowl with the remaining ½ cup of sugar until peaks form. Fold into the eggnog. Serve from a punch bowl and top with freshly grated nutmeg.

AMARO MILK SHAKE

Amaro is a category of European drinking bitters that served the function of stimulating the appetite (*aperitivo*) or encouraging digestion (*digestivo*). Traditionally used either by themselves or in a simple highball with carbonated water, they are nonetheless delightful in mixed drinks, such as this whimsical shake. *Serves 2*

3 ounces Ramazzotti or other amaro, such as Averna or Fernet Branca

4 ounces whole milk

1 pint French vanilla ice cream

Place the liquid ingredients in a blender pitcher, then add the ice cream. Blend until the desired consistency is achieved. Pour into frozen parfait glasses and serve with straws.

GOLDEN SLEIGH

This cocktail is a holiday variation on the classic Golden Cadillac, substituting eggnog for the heavy cream. It is a member of the Grasshopper family, from which I seem to have been separated at birth.

1 ounce Galliano

1 ounce white crème de cacao

2 ounces eggnog

Freshly grated nutmeg, for garnish

Combine the Galliano, crème de cacao, and eggnog in a mixing glass and shake vigorously with ice to chill. Strain into a chilled coupe glass and garnish with freshly grated nutmeg.

KELLY RAILEAN

RAILEAN DISTILLING

Just southeast of Houston on the Gulf of Mexico lies the sleepy town of San Leon. Self-described as "a small drinking community with a large fishing problem," San Leon is home to Eagle Point Distillery, where rum maven Kelly Railean plies her trade.

For over a decade, Railean worked in nearby Houston, distributing fine wines to restaurants and clubs. In the 1990s she and her husband, Matt, caught the sailing bug, and they began sailing extensively on Galveston Bay and eventually throughout the Caribbean. It was on their sailing trips that they began to learn about pirate lore and by extension they began drinking and collecting rum. As their rum collection grew, Kelly had the idea to start a rum distillery in Texas.

In 2006, she went all-in. Their rum releases include both unaged and aged rums, as well as a spiced rum. No colors or flavors are added to any of its products, and all ingredients are sourced entirely from the United States. Furthermore, Railean's is one of very few spirits to carry the "Made in USA" certification, assuring that every product that carries the Railean label is fermented, distilled, aged, and bottled by hand on American soil from American components. San Leon is home to a colony of monk parakeets, and these green birds grace the label of every bottle that comes out of the Eagle Point Distillery.

HOR-VETTE

San Antonio bartender Matt Moody created this beguiling and contradictory concoction to be a dessert in liquid form. Elegant French liqueur combines with the rustic rice beverage of Mexico. If you don't make the horchata yourself, pick up a quart to go from your favorite taqueria, but make sure you're using a fresh product—avoid the powdered stuff.

3 ounces Bartender's Easy Horchata
(recipe follows)
1 ounce Crème Yvette
Strip of grapefruit zest, for garnish

Build the liquid ingredients in an ice-filled Old Fashioned glass and garnish with the grapefruit zest.

BARTENDER'S EASY HORCHATA

Many horchata recipes require special equipment and advanced planning. For those who prefer to do things on the fly, here is a quick horchata recipe that can be completed in under an hour. Horchata is great on its own, and also makes for a great substitution for milk in coffee drinks, and, of course, plays well with spirits. *Makes 1 quart*

1 cup white rice

2 cinnamon sticks

2 star anise

6½ cups water

Pinch of salt

2½ cups whole milk

1 (14-ounce) can sweetened condensed milk

3 teaspoons vanilla extract

2 ounces Orgeat *(page 109)*

4 ounces Canela Syrup *(page 59)*

In a large, dry sauté pan, toast the rice with the whole spices for a few minutes over medium heat until a nutty aroma emerges. In the meantime, bring 2 cups of the water to a boil in a kettle. Once the rice is thoroughly heated and just starting to brown, add the hot water to the pan. Bring to a boil, then cover and turn off the heat. Once the rice is cooked, remove the spices from the pan and discard. Transfer the cooked rice to a blender pitcher. Add the salt, 2¼ cups of the remaining water, and 1¼ cups of the whole milk to the pitcher and blend thoroughly. Strain through a fine-mesh strainer into another large container. Add the remaining 2¼ cups of water and 1¼ cups of whole milk, and the sweetened condensed milk, vanilla, orgeat, and *canela* syrup. Stir the ingredients with a whisk. Taste and adjust the seasonings as needed. Store refrigerated for up to 1 week.

IRISH COFFEE

San Francisco's Buena Vista Café is the spiritual homeland of Irish Coffee in the United States. It is at once one of the most delicious cocktails (when made properly) and one of the most disastrous (when made poorly) in the book. At its best, it is the perfect cold weather warmer—a contrast of sweet, hot, boozy coffee sipped through cold, rich, fatty cream. When made haphazardly—incorporating Irish Cream, crème de menthe, aerosol whipped cream, or a host of other inappropriate ingredients—it is a tremendous disappointment. One conspirator in the poor manufacture of Irish Coffee is the so-called Irish Coffee mug, that footed glass mug that so many people somehow came to the conclusion they couldn't live without. Whatever they may be good for, Irish Coffee is not it. The traditional tulip-shaped Irish Coffee glass is both proportioned and shaped correctly such as to encourage proper preparation; a small wineglass (the size for white wine) will also suffice. The coffee should be hot, fresh, and strong. The cream should be thickened but still pourable, so that it will sit nicely on top of the hot coffee, allowing the drink to layer, such that the components come together only in the drinker's mouth.

3 ounces unsweetened heavy cream *(do not substitute half-and-half)*

1 ounce Simple Syrup *(page 83)*

1½ ounces Irish whiskey, such as Tullamore Dew

4 ounces hot black coffee

First, prepare the cream. Use a whisk in a bowl, or shake the cream inside a Boston shaker. Don't overdo it, however, as the cream will thicken quickly.

Place the simple syrup and whiskey in a glass and slowly pour in the hot coffee. Pour the heavy cream over the back of a spoon to float. The finished drink should look like a glass of Guinness, with the cream serving as the "head."

VELVET HAMMER

The Velvet Hammer is one of those good-natured members of the Alexander family. For an even more luxurious treat, substitute a scoop of vanilla ice cream for the heavy cream.

2 ounces Texas vodka

1 ounce white crème de cacao

¾ ounce Paula's Texas Orange or Cointreau

2 ounces heavy cream

Freshly grated nutmeg, for garnish

Combine all the liquid ingredients in a mixing glass and shake vigorously with ice to chill. Strain into a chilled coupe or Martini-style glass. Dust with grated nutmeg, if desired.

METRIC CONVERSIONS AND EQUIVALENTS

Metric Conversion Formulas

Ounces to grams . . . . *multiply* . . . . Ounces by 28.35

Pounds to kilograms . . . . *multiply* . . . . Pounds by 0.454

Teaspoons to milliliters . . . . *multiply* . . . . Teaspoons by 4.93

Tablespoons to milliliters . . . . *multiply* . . . . Tablespoons by 14.79

Fluid ounces to milliliters . . . . *multiply* . . . . Fluid ounces by 29.57

Cups to milliliters . . . . *multiply* . . . . Cups by 236.59

Cups to liters . . . . *multiply* . . . . Cups by 0.236

Pints to liters . . . . *multiply* . . . . Pints by 0.473

Quarts to liters . . . . *multiply* . . . . Quarts by 0.946

Gallons to liters . . . . *multiply* . . . . Gallons by 3.785

Inches to centimeters . . . . *multiply* . . . . Inches by 2.54

Approximate Metric Equivalents Weight

¼ ounce .7 grams	3 ounces. . . . . .85 grams
½ ounce . . . . .14 grams	4 ounces (¼ pound). . . . . 113 grams
¾ ounce . . . . .21 grams	5 ounces. . . . . .142 grams
1 ounce. . . . . 28 grams	6 ounces . . . . .170 grams
1¼ ounces. . . . . .35 grams	7 ounces . . . . .198 grams
1½ ounces . . . . 42.5 grams	8 ounces (½ pound) . . . . .227 grams
1⅔ ounces. . . . . .45 grams	16 ounces (1 pound) . . . . .454 grams
2 ounces. . . . . .57 grams	35.25 ounces (2.2 pounds) . . . . 1 kilogram

Approximate Metric Equivalents Volume

¼ teaspoon . . . . .1 milliliter	½ cup (4 fluid ounces) . . . . . .120 milliliters
½ teaspoon . . . . 2.5 milliliters	⅔ cup . . . . 160 milliliters
¾ teaspoon . . . . .4 milliliters	¾ cup . . . . .180 milliliters
1 teaspoon . . . . .5 milliliters	1 cup (8 fluid ounces) . . . . . 240 milliliters
1¼ teaspoons . . . . 6 milliliters	1¼ cups . . . . 300 milliliters
1½ teaspoons . . . . .7.5 milliliters	1½ cups (12 fluid ounces) . . . 360 milliliters
1¾ teaspoons . . . . 8.5 milliliters	1⅔ cups . . . . 400 milliliters
2 teaspoons . . . . .10 milliliters	2 cups (1 pint) . . . . 460 milliliters
1 tablespoon (½ fluid ounce) . . 15 milliliters	3 cups . . . . 700 milliliters
2 tablespoons (1 fluid ounce) . . 30 milliliters	4 cups (1 quart) . . . . .0.95 liter
¼ cup . . . . 60 milliliters	1 quart plus ¼ cup . . . . .1 liter
⅓ cup . . . . 80 milliliters	4 quarts (1 gallon) . . . . 3.8 liters

Approximate Metric Equivalents Length

⅛ inch . . . . .3 millimeters	2½ inches . . . . 6 centimeters
¼ inch . . . . .6 millimeters	4 inches . . . . .10 centimeters
½ inch . . . . 1.25 centimeters	5 inches . . . . .13 centimeters
1 inch . . . . 2.5 centimeters	6 inches . . . . .15.25 centimeters
2 inches . . . . .5 centimeters	12 inches (1 foot) . . . . 30 centimeters

Information compiled from a variety of sources, including Recipes into Type *by Joan Whitman and Dolores Simon (Newton, MA: Biscuit Books, 2000);* The New Food Lover's Companion *by Sharon Tyler Herbst (Hauppauge, NY: Barron's, 1995); and* Rosemary Brown's Big Kitchen Instruction Book *(Kansas City, MO: Andrews McMeel, 1998).*

ACKNOWLEDGMENTS

They say it's not a good idea to drink alone, and the same should be said about putting together a cocktail book. I'd like to thank Kirsty Melville and Jean Lucas at Andrews McMeel for recognizing that Texas has something to say about cocktails and spirits, and being willing to put their best effort behind that idea. Thanks to Martha Hopkins for convincing me to do this in the first place; and thanks to her Terrace Partners cohort Randall Lockridge for the sexy book design.

This book would not have been possible without the team of Tipsy Texans: Matt Moody, who tested recipes with me into the wee hours; Justin Esquivel, the designer who makes us look classier than we actually are; Michael Thad Carter, who is not afraid to break a sweat capturing a fresh portrait; Aimee Wenske, who shot scores and scores of drinks, and thankfully ignored my recommendation that she drink them all; Kate LeSueur for her special touches; and chief cheerleader and whip-cracker, the multitalented Crystal Esquivel. This book would not have existed without her editorial talent and her strict wrangling of my iPhone calendar.

Thank you to all the bartenders, journalists, and industry colleagues who contributed to this effort in particular, and to our community in general—your friendship is almost as important to me as all that tasty booze: Bill Norris, Adam Harris, Lara Nixon, Jason Stevens, Sean Connor, Ann Tuennerman, Adam Bryan, Jeret Peña, MM Pack, Matt Tanner, Claudia Alarcón, Tomas Estes, David Suro, Bobby Heugel, Alba Huerta, Nate Wales, Pam Prichard, Chris Bostick, Beth Bellanti-Walker, Houston Eaves, Lucinda Hutson, Jenny Rabb, Kevin Smothers, and the entire USBG. Thanks to Marla and Jenna at Edible Austin; Addie Broyles, Michael Barnes, and Emma Janzen at the *Austin American-Statesman*; Virginia Wood and Wes Marshall at the *Austin Chronicle*; and Jennifer McInnis at the *San Antonio Express-News*. Special thanks to everyone at Twin Liquors for their continued support.

And to my drinking buddies and dearest friends, a toast: to the Crowls, the Smalleys, the Sharps, the Duple-Mahrers, the Sanderses, Joe and Quinn, Jenny and Mike, Philip Cochran, Mom, Dad, Sister, and baby Django. And to Joe, whose amusing antics brighten my days and make me feel like I have my own court jester, despite my commoner status.

INDEX